# LORD OF THE
# COSMOS

# LORD OF THE
# COSMOS

## MITHRAS, PAUL, AND
## THE GOSPEL OF MARK

### MICHAEL PATELLA

t&t clark

NEW YORK • LONDON

T & T Clark International, 80 Maiden Lane, New York, NY 10038

T & T Clark International, The Tower Building, 11 York Road, London SE1 7NX

T & T Clark International is a Continuum imprint.

Unless otherwise indicated, Scripture texts in this work are from the *New American Bible with Revised New Testament and Revised Psalms* © 1991, 1986, 1970 Confraternity of Christian Doctrine, Washington, DC, and are used by permission of the copyright owner; all rights reserved.

NRSV indicates quotation from the *New Revised Standard Version Bible*, copyright 1989, by the Division of Christian Education of the National Council of the Churches of Christ in the USA, and used by permission.

Cover art: Mithras immolating the bull. Double face relief (2nd–3rd CE). Louvre, Paris, France. Erich Lessing / Art Resource, NY.

Cover design: Brenda Klinger

**Library of Congress Cataloging-in-Publication Data**

Patella, Michael, 1954–
    Lord of the cosmos : Mithras, Paul, and the gospel of Mark / Michael Patella.
        p.   cm.
    Includes bibliographical references and index.
    ISBN 0–567–02522–5 (hardcover) – ISBN 0–567–02532–2 (pbk.)
    1. Mithraism – Influence. 2. Bible. N.T. Mark – Theology. 3. Bible. N.T. Epistles of Paul – Theology. 4. Bible. N.T. Mark – Relation to the Epistles of Paul. 5. Bible. N.T. Epistles of Paul – Relation to Mark.   I. Title.
    BS2585.52.P37 2006
    225.6'7 – dc22

                                                                                            2006001135

*Printed in the United States of America*

06   07   08   09   10              10   9   8   7   6   5   4   3   2   1

*For the three graces,*
*Alma Pavia*
*Viola Campagna*
*Anne Patella*

# Contents

# Acknowledgments

The Task Force on Mark, which gathered each summer since 1998 at the annual meeting of The Catholic Biblical Association of America, not only provided the impetus for this work; it also sustained an ongoing critique of its development. I give thanks also to Justin Taylor, S.M., for proposing a number of improvements to the manuscript, to Angela del Greco for helping prepare the final draft, to the brothers of the Society of Saint John the Evangelist in Cambridge, Massachusetts, for their hospitality and welcome, and to Ursula Klie for her interest and encouragement. And to Amy Wagner and her editorial staff.

My gratitude goes to Abbot John Klassen, O.S.B., of Saint John's Abbey and to President Dietrich Reinhart, O.S.B., of Saint John's University, who granted me a year-long sabbatical for completing the research, to my colleagues at Saint John's University and the College of Saint Benedict for their input at the Collegial Conversations presentation, to my monastic confreres who have always furnished so much fraternal support. And to my mother, who died as this book went to press, I owe everything.

# Abbreviations

Abbreviations for biblical and deuterocanonical books and for ancient literature conform to *The SBL Handbook of Style*. Peabody, MA: Hendrickson, 1999.

| | |
|---|---|
| // | parallel to |
| A.J. | Josephus, *Jewish Antiquities* |
| ANRW | *Aufstieg und Niedergang der römischen Welt: Geschichte und Kultur Roms im Spiegel der neueren Forschung.* Edited by H. Temporini and W. Haase. Berlin, 1972– |
| BAR | *Biblical Archaeology Review* |
| Bib | *Biblica* |
| B.J. | Josephus, *Jewish War* |
| CahRB | Cahiers de la Revue biblique |
| CBQ | *Catholic Biblical Quarterly* |
| ÉBib | *Études bibliques* |
| ÉPRO | Études preliminaries aux religions orientales dans l'empire romain |
| JBL | *Journal of Biblical Literature* |
| JMS | *Journal of Mithraic Studies* |
| LCL | Loeb Classical Library |
| LXX | Greek Old Testament, with references enclosed in square brackets when different from NRSV versification |
| LTUR | *Lexicon topographicum urbis Romae.* Edited by Eva Margareta Steinby. 6 vols. Rome: Edizioni Quasar, 1993–2000 |
| MT | Masoretic Text of the Hebrew Bible, with references enclosed in square brackets when different from NRSV versification |

NAB          New American Bible (see copyright page), with references enclosed in square brackets when different from NRSV versification

*NovT*        *Novum Testamentum*

NRSV        New Revised Standard Version (see copyright page)

*NTS*         *New Testament Studies*

NTTS        New Testament Tools and Studies

OT           Old Testament

pass. ptc.   passive participle

*RB*          *Revue biblique*

SBLDS      Society of Biblical Literature Dissertation Series

SP           Sacred Pagina

*ST*          *Studia theological*; suppl. supplementary

*TDNT*       *Theological Dictionary of the New Testament*. Edited by G. Kittel and G. Friedrich. Translated by G. W. Bromiley. 10 vols. Grand Rapids, 1964–76

WUNT       Wissenschaftliche Untersuchungen zum Alten und Neuen Testament

# Introduction

Mark's Gospel presents Jesus as the Son of God, who battles Satan and reclaims and redeems creation from him. This ongoing battle is evident within the earthly ministry and reaches its climax and decisive victory in the passion, death, and resurrection. Jesus conquers death, and disciples who enter into his life through baptism share in his triumph and gain eternal life. Insofar as Mark evidences this participationist theology of Jesus' life, we can see a strong Pauline character to Mark's Gospel.

Mark's Gospel resonated in the imperial capital and beyond because its inherent participationist theology, probably augmented by Paul and possibly introduced by him, touched important issues in Rome. Furthermore, it adhered to these issues by employing the language and thought of the ancient world. The foundation of this philosophy was Plato's *Timaeus*, a work that supplied the astronomical support for the astrological interpretation prevalent in the intertestamental period. Mithraism, which became the most popular astrological system at that time, was interpreted within this Platonic framework. Mithraism moved from the eastern regions of the Roman Empire into the heart of Rome itself. Although it did not rise to such prominence in the city until fifty to one hundred years after the writing of Mark's Gospel, its major currents of thought took root in the Markan community through Paul's contact with Rome. The principal component inherent in Mark is its cosmology. Jews and God-fearing Gentiles, influenced by the cultural currents in the ancient imperial city of Rome, would find in Mark a message allowing them access to the Christian mystery, and in so doing would unite themselves to the eternal, one God.

A concentrated reading of Mark's Gospel yields several points that reflect the ancient cosmology along with a challenge to it. In this first chapter, we establish the cosmology that influenced early Christianity. The second chapter draws connections between Pauline and Markan treatment of this cosmology, and chapter 3 demonstrates how Mark interprets the ancient worldview in light of Jesus' passion, death, and resurrection.

Many studies have taken up the topic of various Hellenistic mystery religions and their influence on the Gospels, particularly over the twentieth century.[1] The

---

1. Richard S. Ascough (*What Are They Saying about the Formation of Pauline Churches?* [New York: Paulist Press, 1998], 50–99) gives a broad, concise, and helpful overview of the major scholarly works that have addressed the mystery religions and their role in the development of Christianity.

prevailing opinions break down into two camps. The first sees the Gospels and Christianity as an adaptation and offshoot of the cults of Dionysus, Cybele and Attis, Isis and Osiris, Mithras, and others.[2] The second camp holds that there has not been any such infiltration of mystery cults within Christianity.[3]

Rather than try to prove or disprove a direct influence of Mithraism on the Gospels, however, it is more accurate to speak about the world and culture that Christianity and Mithras share and reflect. Several reasons support this approach.

Above all, no documents from the Mithraic cult exist. Until they come to light, if ever they do, to draw definitive conclusions about the Mithraic mysteries and Gospel formation is speculation at best. In addition, the terms "Mithras" or "Perseus" do not appear in any language of any canonical version of Scripture, nor are they evident in those Gnostic texts often seen as having some bearing on Christianity, such as the *Gospel of Peter,* the *Gospel of Thomas,* or the *Sayings of Thomas.* To find veiled Mithraic references in canonical or noncanonical Christian texts, therefore, is impossible, or at least quite difficult to substantiate.

The greatest source for understanding Mithraism lies in the archaeological record. On this level, evidence of Mithraism is ubiquitous throughout the ancient Roman world. Even here, however, the mithraea in the city of Rome postdate the formation of Mark's Gospel by at least fifty to one hundred years.[4] A most

---

2. Wilhelm Bousset, *Kyrios Christos* (Nashville: Abingdon, 1970); Rudolf Bultmann, *Primitive Christianity in Its Contemporary Setting* (London: Thames & Hudson, 1956); Alfred Loisy, *Les mystère païens et le mystère chrétien* (Paris: Emile Nourry, 1914); Richard Reitzenstein, *Hellenistic Mystery-Religions: Their Basic Ideas and Significance* (trans. John E. Steely; Pittsburgh: Pickwick, 1978).

3. Bruce M. Metzger, "Methodology in the Study of the Mystery Religions and Early Christianity," in *Historical and Literary Studies: Pagan, Jewish, and Christian* (NTTS 8; Grand Rapids: Eerdmanns, 1968), 1–24; A. D. Nock, "Early Gentile Christianity and Its Hellenistic Background," in *Essays on Religion and the Ancient World* (ed. Zeph Stewart; Cambridge, MA: Harvard University Press, 1972), 49–133; idem, "Hellenistic Mysteries and Christian Sacraments," in *Essays,* 791–820; idem, "The Vocabulary of the New Testament," in *Essays,* 341–47; Günther Wagner, *Pauline Baptism and the Pagan Mysteries: The Problem of the Pauline Doctrine of Baptism in Romans VI, 1–11, in the Light of Its Religio-Historical "Parallels"* (Edinburgh: Oliver & Boyd, 1967); A. J. M. Wedderburn, "Paul and the Hellenistic Mystery-Cults: On Posing the Right Questions," in *La soteriologia dei culti orientali nell'Impero romano: Atti dei Colloquio internazionale su la soteriologia dei culti orientali nell'Impero romano, Roma 24–28 Settembre 1979* (ed. Ugo Bianchi and Maarten J. Vermaseren; ÉPRO 92; Leiden: Brill, 1982), 817–33; idem, "Hellenistic Christian Traditions in Romans 6?" *NTS* 29 (1983): 337–55; idem, *Baptism and Resurrection: Studies in Pauline Theology against Its Graeco-Roman Background* (WUNT 44; Tübingen: Mohr [Siebeck], 1987); idem, "The Soteriology of the Mysteries and Pauline Baptismal Theology," *NovT* 29 (1987): 53–72.

4. E. Lissi Caronna, "Castra Peregrina," *LTUR* 1:249–50; idem, "Castra Peregrina: Mithraeum," 1:251; I. della Giovampaolo, "Mitra (S. Clemens; Reg. II)," *LTUR* 3:257–59; J. Calzini Gysens, "Aedes Herculis et Dionysii," *LTUR* 3:262; idem, "Arx," 3:265–66; idem, "Domus Augustana," 3:266; idem, "Domus: Nummi," 3:262; idem, "Emporium," 3:270; idem, "Facoltà di Ingegneria," 3:260; idem, "Horti Lamiani," 3:261; idem, "Horti Sallustiani," 3:264; idem, "M. degli Olympii, S. Silvestro in Capite," 3:264–65; idem, "Mithra," 3:257; idem, "Ospedale di San Giovanni sul Celio," 3:261–62; idem, "Palazzo Barberini," 3:263–64; idem, "Palazzo della Cancelleria Apostolica," 3:266; idem, "S. Saba," 3:269; idem, "Spelaeum in Via G. Lanza," 3:260–61; idem, "Spelaeum nel foro di Nerva," 3:265; idem, "Thermae Titi," 3:260; idem, "Via Mazzarino," 3:263; idem, "Via Passalacqua," 3:259–60;

important point for our purposes, however, is that Mithraism appears in the eastern regions of the empire much earlier.

If we consider that Mithraism contains important elements described in Plato's *Timaeus*, we must deal seriously with the possibility that language and thought of such a worldview existed among the inhabitants of the intertestamental period, Jews and Christians included. In addition, writings of the earliest Christian communities could evidence these thoughts and use certain vocabulary to do so. This study, concentrating on the Gospel of Mark, for reasons discussed below, will look to Paul's influence on the early Christian community in Rome and his role in "Christianizing" Mithraic concepts and language for that community.

Before taking this subject any further, however, we must acknowledge the pitfalls of such a study.

## *Methodological Approach*

The great variety of opinion on the role mystery cults have played in early Christianity is in large part the result of erroneous assumptions. A. J. M. Wedderburn addresses this problem.[5] The difficulty is that many who compare the practices and beliefs of early Christianity either to Gnosticism or the mystery cults tend to think that every similarity between the two is the result of Christian borrowing from the non-Christian or pagan belief; such scholars will not allow the fact that Christianity may well have influenced the non-Christian religions. So, for example, Christianity may tell us more about the beginnings of Gnosticism than Gnosticism tells us about Christian origins.

Wedderburn distinguishes Gnosticism from the mystery cults.[6] The latter were rivals to Christianity, and Mithraism was the greatest competitor, but the same cannot be said about Gnosticism. Nonetheless, we cannot expect that the competing claims of Christianity never touched the mystery cults, nor can we think that Christianity was never influenced by them. The question to ask is, How early does this mutual exchange take place?[7] It is impossible to answer the question with exactitude, however, because, as Wedderburn observes, without a corresponding discovery like Qumran or Nag Hammadi, we will never learn more about the

---

idem, "Vigna Muti," 3:262–63; idem, "Vigne e Magarozzi," 3:259; idem, "Villa Giustiniani-Massimo," 3:261; M. Andreussi, "Mitra (S. Prisca; Reg. XIII)," *LTUR* 3:268–69; C. Lega, "S. Sabina," *LTUR* 3:269–70; M. Piranomante, "Spelunga," *LTUR* 3:267–68; A. M. Ramieri, "Antrum," *LTUR* 3:266–67. The city of Rome's ancient port, Ostia, numbers eighteen mithraea, all from Hadrian's reign, 117–138 CE (*Guida d'Italia del Touring Club Italiano* [Milan: Artistico-Letteraria del T.C.I., 1979], 627, 630).

5. Wedderburn, "Paul," 817–33.

6. Ibid., 822.

7. Ibid.

mystery cults than we already know.[8] Outside of archaeological remains and inscriptions, there is no way to uncover what the mystery cults actually believed.
Their practices were not for the general public to know.

The secrecy notwithstanding, Wedderburn observes that "much of their views
and language did filter through to the world around them[,] and the views and
language of the world around ... [were] taken up and used by them, and it is this
common religious and philosophical culture, rather than the differentia of the
mystery cults[,] which is the most fruitful source of enquiry."[9]

Wedderburn concludes with four caveats in any discussion on the relation
between Paul and the mystery cults.[10] Research in this area should

♦ not treat these cults in isolation from the whole culture of which they were
  part, but allow for their influence on, and being influence by, that culture;

♦ not treat Paul's theology in isolation from the Christian heritage that he used
  and adapted, but reckon with various substrata of tradition used by him that
  may have differed from him in certain respects;

♦ not ignore the possibility that to react against something is to be influenced
  by it no less than if one adopts it as one's own;

♦ not ignore the possibility that, even if the whole of Paul's thought in a passage
  like Rom 6 is not influenced by the mysteries, parts of it, individual motifs or
  ideas, may well be, directly or directly.

In a separate study based on the approach outlined above, Wedderburn compares and contrasts Pauline baptism with initiatory rites of the mystery cults.[11]
Although he does not take up the Mithraic cult as such, the conclusions he
reaches are still applicable in this case.

In many of the mystery cults, it appears on the surface that initiates "shared in
the sufferings of a dying and rising god."[12] Wedderburn, however, demonstrates
that this assumption is false. For example, in the cult of Isis and Osiris, initiates
would undergo many washings and abstinence, approach the boundary of death,
worship the gods below and above; but they would never share in Isis' search for
the murdered Osiris, or share in Isis' rejoicing upon finding him. Their proximity
to the gods would permit them to have communion with them. In the end,
the initiates would emerge before the crowds of worshippers in dress suggesting
a divine status. Yet for the initiates, as Wedderburn points out, "this change

---

8. Ibid., 829.
9. Ibid.
10. Ibid.
11. Wedderburn ("Soteriology," 53–72) investigates the cult of Isis and Osiris, the Eleusinian
Mysteries, the Dionysiac rites, and the Cybele and Attis cult.
12. Ibid., 57.

should be seen as one of status rather than a transformation of [their] nature."[13] Wedderburn shows similar patterns in the cults of the Eleusinian Mysteries, of Dionysius, and of Cybele and Attis.[14]

Wedderburn sees the Christian soteriological understanding as much different from the ones offered by the mystery cults. In the mystery cults, the worshippers are not conformed to the suffering, dying, or rising of the deity in their ritual, even less so in their lives outside the confines of religious ritual. In Christian soteriology, as outlined in passages like Rom 6 and 2 Cor 5:14–15, however, believers enter into the life, death, and resurrection of the Deity, Christ.[15] We can add to Wedderburn's study that the Gospel of Mark offers a similar understanding of the life and death of Christ. In addition, his procedure can also be applied to Mithraism.

---

13. Ibid., 58.
14. Ibid., 62–71.
15. Ibid., 56–57.

*Part One*

# The Cosmological Context of Paul and Mark

## Chapter 1

# Hellenistic Cosmology

### *Timaeus*

The foundational work for understanding the Greco-Roman view of the cosmos is Plato's *Timaeus*. Containing elements of mathematics, astronomy, and philosophy, the *Timaeus* features a sustained and thorough discussion of the state of the universe. The protagonist, Timaeus, sees the cosmos resulting from the combination of necessity with reason,[1] which he further on refers to as "causes."[2] He equates "reason" with the "divine" and claims that in order to achieve a life of blessedness, one ought to pursue the divine. Hence, seeking after necessity becomes the preferred means to achieving this union.[3]

Timaeus then reiterates the point that all things were chaos until God placed them in harmony and proportion to each other. The balance and harmony that God instigates results in the cosmos, a living creature containing both mortal and immortal living creatures.[4] The mortal creatures, in turn, have received an immortal soul, for which the body is the vehicle.[5] The various cults that flourished in the Hellenistic world supported this understanding in one form or another, and it is not altogether alien to major parts of Christian belief.

### *Mithraism*

Of all the Hellenistic cults that influenced or were influenced by Christianity, Mithraism excites the greatest interest. Both Christianity and Mithraism are Oriental religions, and both gained tremendous popularity in the Mediterranean World at approximately the same time. Although the Gospel of Mark was not

---

1. Plato, *Timaeus* 48a; in R. G. Bury, trans., *Plato*, vol. 9, *Timaeus, Critias, Cleitophon, Menexenus, Epistles* (LCL; Cambridge, MA: Harvard University Press, 1989), 108.
2. Ibid., 68e (9:176).
3. Ibid., 68e–69a (9:176–78).
4. Ibid., 69b (9:178).
5. Ibid., 69c–d (9:178–80).

written as apology in the face of Mithraism or attack against it, at the time of its writing it was breathing the same cultural air as Mithraism. Thus, many of the issues Mark addresses would resonate among the Romans.

In general, the intertestamental Mediterranean world saw a movement from a collectivized use of religion to an individuation of religion, the human desire to break free of fate's control over life, and the destabilization of society following the inroads of Hellenism.[6] Both Christianity and Mithraism grew in this soil. Mithraism itself provides a good example of the syncretism that became so prevalent after the conquests of Alexander the Great.

The god Mithras, of Indo-European origin and mentioned at least as early as 1400 BCE in a Hittite Text, was worshiped in both northern India and the Iranian plateau.[7] Within Persian circles, Mithras is a warrior who becomes allied with the Iranian god Ahura Mazda in his ongoing battle with the evil god Ahriman; Mithras is often depicted bringing life to the earth by killing the cosmic bull.[8] By 400 BCE, Mithras became closely associated with the royal house of the Persian Empire.[9]

As Persia swept through the Mesopotamian River Valley, the Fertile Crescent, and Asia Minor, Babylonian and Chaldean astrological and eschatological elements adhered to Mithras; the *magi* of the Zaruthustrian reform became missionaries for the cult.[10] Once Mithraism entered the cultural orbit of Greece and Rome, elements of Hellenistic mystery religions began to adhere to it.[11] One of the earliest notices and in this study's case the most pertinent report about Mithras comes from Plutarch, who writes, around 67 CE, that Cilician pirates practiced the cult.[12] Through trading and governmental circles, the cult spread from Palestine to Britain, and the god Mithras became the guardian of the Roman legions, with over one hundred mithraea in Rome alone.[13] Commodus (180–192 CE) was initiated into the cult, and a half a century later, Diocletian (243–316) declared Mithras a state god and "guardian of the Empire."[14]

---

6. Gary Lease, "Mithraism and Christianity: Borrowings and Transformations," in *ANRW,* Part 2, *Principat,* 23.2 (1980): 1309.

7. Lease (ibid., 1310) bases his findings predominantly on Maarten J. Vermaseren, *Mithras, Geschichte eines Kultes* (Stuttgart: W. Kohlhammer, 1965), as well as Hugo Gressmann, *Die orientalischen Religionen im hellenistisch-römischen Zeitalter* (Berlin: de Gruyter, 1930).

8. Lease, "Mithraism," 1310.

9. Ibid.

10. Ibid.

11. Ibid.

12. Ibid.

13. Ibid., 1310–11.

14. Lease (ibid.) bases his finding on Franz Cumont, *The Mysteries of Mithra* (New York: Dover, 1956), as well as Vermaseren, *Mithras.*

Mithraism has left many archaeological remains, and a few patristic writers mention it in their texts.[15] Yet until most recently, no one had been able to crack the symbol system of the cult.[16] Heretofore, the accepted understanding has been that Mithras, born from a rock, is commanded by the sun god to recapture a bull who previously had escaped Mithras's grasp.[17] Mithras does so, but this time he mounts the bull on its right side, clenches it by the nose, and kills it with a stab wound to the neck.[18] A new creation comes through the death of the bull.[19] Gary Lease, M. J. Vermaseren, and others variously interpret the symbolism of the attendant animals. The dog is Mithras's hunting companion, who along with the snake is a Persian symbol of goodness and who licks the bull's blood.[20] The scorpion, a servant of the Iranian god of evil, Ahriman, tries to poison the bull's sperm by stinging its testicles, thereby cursing all animals descending from the new creation engendered by the bull's death.[21]

The iconography nearly always features the sun, moon, planets, four seasons, and other cosmological depictions. In fact, the myth includes an eschatological battle in which Mithras conquers the sun god, Helios, and the two share a cultic meal together, the conclusion of which sees both Mithras and Helios riding to heaven in the sun god's quadriga.[22] In a final battle at the end of the world, Mithras vanquishes Ahriman and his minions and ushers in the resurrection of the dead by bringing their souls into the highest sphere of the stars.[23]

Because Mithraism was a mystery cult, little is known about its initiation rites and practices. A statue or carving of Mithras slaying the bull is always in a prominent position in nearly all mithraea.[24] A mithraeum was most often situated in a cave, and where none was available, a windowless lower or upper room was built.[25] In any case, there was only one entrance, and some archaeological remains suggest something akin to a baptistery.[26] Evidence of a triclinium in these

---

15. Justin Martyr, *Dialogue with Trypho* 1; 70; 78; idem, *Apology 1*, 66; Gregory of Nazianzus, *Oratio* 4; Tertullian, *De baptismo* 5; idem, *De corona militis* 15; idem, *De praescriptione haereticorum* 40; Origen, *Contra Celsum* 6,22.

16. David Ulansey, *The Origins of the Mithraic Mysteries* (New York: Oxford University Press, 1989), does explain the symbol system; his discoveries are discussed below.

17. Lease, "Mithraism," 1311.

18. Ibid.

19. Ibid.

20. Ibid.

21. Ibid.

22. Ibid., 1312.

23. Ibid.

24. Ibid.

25. Ibid.

26. Ibid.

caves or rooms indicates that some kind of cultic meal took place, which texts suggest as consisting of bread, water, honey, and wine.[27]

Initiates had difficult tests to undergo, including a branding that precluded a follower from accepting any crown.[28] Disciples of Mithras were all brothers, and Mithras himself was a *comes*, or intimate friend, and not merely a distant god.[29] By emulating Mithras through the cultic rites, followers would gain eternal salvation; furthermore, they would find in Mithras a model for human, moral life.[30]

## Mithraism, a Cosmology

The Mithraic mysteries have continued to puzzle scholars despite the research of Franz Cumont, Hugo Gressmann, Lease, Vermaseren and others. The subterranean construction of many of the Mithraic worship spaces guaranteed the preservation of their frescoes, many of which are in remarkable condition. This last detail is most important for our purposes.

In any mithraeum, the central focus is either a painting or sculpture of a tauroctony where a young man, usually in a cape, slays a bull by thrusting a knife into the beast's neck or shoulder. The nineteenth-century German scholar Karl B. Stark held that the paintings surrounding this young man depicted not Iranian gods, as some had suggested, but heavenly constellations.[31] David Ulansey, following the findings of Stark, Alessandro Bausani, Roger Beck, Stanley Insler, and Michael Speidel, agrees that the Mithraic tauroctony is a star map representing various constellations, but he claims that the young man performing the slaying has no astral identification. Furthermore, in relation to the other constellations, if the bull is supposed to represent Taurus, it is out of its calendrical place.[32] Ulansey concludes, however, that the Taurus's misplacement, when read alongside the identity of Mithras, forms the key to understanding the whole Mithraic religious system.

---

27. Ibid.

28. Lease (ibid.) bases his conclusions on Tertullian, *De corona* 15.

29. Lease (ibid.) bases his findings on Günther Haufe, "Die Mysterien," in *Umwelt des Urchristentums*, vol. 1, *Darstellung des neutestamentlichen Zeitalters* (ed. J. Leipoldt and W. Grundmann; Berlin: Evangelische Verlagsanstalt, 1975), 101–26.

30. Lease, "Mithraism," 1312.

31. Karl B. Stark, *Zwei Mithräen der grossherzoglichen Alterthümersammlung in Karlsruhe* (Heidelberg, 1865).

32. Ulansey, *Origins*, 3–14. See also Alessandro Bausani, "Note sulla preistoria astronomica del mito di Mithra," in *Mysteria Mithrae* (ed. Ugo Bianchi; Leiden: Brill, 1980), 503–15; Roger Beck, "Cautes and Cautopates: Some Astronomical Considerations," *JMS* 1, no. 2 (1976): 10; idem, "A Note on the Scorpion in the Tauroctony," *JMS* 1, no. 2 (1976): 209; Stanley Insler, "A New Interpretation of the Bull-Slaying Motif," in *Hommages à Maarten J. Vermaseren* (ed. M. B. de Boer and T. A. Edridge; Leiden: Brill, 1978), 523; Michael Speidel, *Mithras-Orion* (Leiden: Brill, 1980), 18.

Although of Persian origin, Mithras was for the Romans syncretistically related with the Greek god Perseus.[33] Both Mithras and Perseus were connected to underground caverns, both have a connection to Persia, and both are portrayed with a curved scythe in hand. Moreover, during the Greco-Roman period, the constellation Perseus appeared above Taurus, a point that links the bull-slaying Mithras to Perseus. Ulansey concludes that the tauroctony in all the mithraea is, therefore, a star map.[34] Furthermore, Ulansey shows that there was a cult of Perseus in the ancient world, centered on the city of Tarsus in Cilicia, the very place which, based on Plutarch, also saw the origin of Mithraism.[35]

Astronomy also helps determine the meaning of the Mithras cult. Ancient stargazers observed the movements of the earth's equator, the celestial equator, and the ecliptic (sun's apparent path through the zodiac). The celestial equator is the imaginary circle produced by the projection of the earth's equator onto the celestial sphere, and it stands at an angle of twenty-three degrees to the ecliptic.[36] These two circles intersect at the points of the autumnal and vernal equinoxes.[37] Ulansey draws attention to a reference in Plato's *Timaeus* where the protagonist explains how the creator of the universe or demiurge constructed the cosmos from two circles that he fashioned "in the form of the letter X."[38] Indeed, one of the earliest depictions of Mithras shows a lion-headed man standing on an orb wrapped by two crossing circles.[39]

Central to Ulansey's thesis is the fact that the celestial equator is not stationary but mobile. A wobble in the earth's rotation, called the precession of the equinoxes, causes a slow but progressive change in the orientation of the earth in space.[40] Hence, the points of the equinox move back one constellation of the zodiac every 2,160 years. For instance, currently the spring equinox in the northern hemisphere occurs when the sun is in Pisces. In approximately 150

---

33. Ulansey, *Origins*, 29.

34. Ibid., 26. In the English edition of Manfred Clauss' *Mithras: Kult und Mysterien* (Munich: C. H. Beck'sche Verlagsbuchhandlung, 1990), translator Richard Gordon (*The Roman Cult of Mithras: The God and His Mysteries* [New York: Routledge, 2000]) observes: "Given Clauss' distaste for speculation, I do not think that, had he been writing the first edition now, he would have come to a conclusion much different from the one he expresses in the Foreword; but he would no doubt have discussed the problems involved more fully than he does" (xviii). In that foreword, Clauss states: "The material [on Mithraism] is ruinously incomplete. This fact makes it all the more worthwhile trying to fit the Mysteries into the wider context of Roman cult-practice" (xxi). Clauss, therefore, does not spend much effort investigating the astronomical and astrological significance of the Mithras cult.

35. Ulansey, *Origins*, 40–45.

36. Ibid., 47.

37. Ibid.

38. Ibid.

39. Ibid., 49.

40. Ibid.

years from now, however, the sun will be in Aquarius.[41] In the Greco-Roman period, the spring equinox occurred in the constellation Aries, while the autumnal
equinox was in Libra.[42] More germane to our point is that from approximately
4000 to 2000 BCE the positions for the spring and fall equinoxes were Taurus
and Scorpio, respectively. Ulansey maintains, therefore, that the tauroctony in
the Mithraic iconography represents the period when the equinoxes appeared
in Taurus and Scorpio.[43] Simultaneously, the constellation Perseus, which is
connected to Mithras, appeared above Taurus during the spring equinoxes of
that time.

A star map fashioned during the Greco-Roman period depicts Perseus extending as far down as the Pleiades, which are located on the bull's shoulder, thereby
drawing Perseus into the picture; indeed, the position of the Pleiades in Taurus
matches identically the place where the dagger enters the bull's shoulder in the
Mithraic tauroctony.[44] In this star map, Perseus' left knee comes down on the
bull's right shoulder, the precise spot where Mithras is shown stabbing his dagger
into the animal.[45]

The astronomer who designed this star map, called the *Phaenomena*, is Aratos,
who follows the map of his predecessor, Eudoxos, a contemporary of Plato.[46]
Aratos, a Stoic, was a native of Soli, which according to Ulansey was an important
Cilician town about twenty miles from Tarsus. So famous was Aratos that the
inhabitants of Soli erected a monument in his honor and even stamped his portrait
on their coins.[47]

Tarsus is also the city of the apostle Paul's birth and early life (Acts 21:39;
22:3), and in addition it was home to a great Stoical school whose greatest intellectual was Posidonius (c. 135–50 BCE). Ulansey demonstrates that Posidonius
and his followers believed in a type of astral religion, were quite interested in
astrology, had an interest in astronomical cycles including the "Great Year" (a
period anywhere from 10,800 to 2,484 years in length), and held to an allegorical
interpretation of natural forces personified as gods and heroes. In addition, their
thought reached its prominence at the same time the Mithraic mysteries were taking hold in Tarsus.[48] During this same period, the Greek astronomer Hipparchus

---

41. Ibid., 50.
42. Ibid., 50–51.
43. Ibid., 51.
44. Ibid., 57.
45. Ibid.
46. Ibid.
47. Ibid., 59.
48. Ibid., 69–76.

(c. 190–126 BCE) discovered the precession of the equinoxes about sixty years before the Cilician pirates were practicing Mithraism, according to Plutarch's later reference.[49]

The reader should recall that until Galileo's research with the telescope (in 1609), the geocentric theory of the universe, adhered to by Hipparchus before Ptolemy adopted it, was the accepted scientific understanding. With such a view of creation, the phenomenon known as the precession of the equinoxes would not be seen as resulting from the earth's wobbling, for the earth was considered the centrally fixed point of the universe. Rather, the belief was that the precession stemmed from a shift in the whole cosmos. For these Stoics, Hipparchus's discovery scientifically confirmed all their astral belief and piety.[50]

In Ulansey's opinion, Mithras, who was the god of Tarsus and who was represented by the constellation Perseus, would have been the deity responsible for initiating the precession of the equinoxes. Perseus' position above Taurus, with his left knee on the bull as he plunges the dagger into the bull's right shoulder, initiates the cosmic shift of the celestial equator so that, in the intertestamental period, the spring equinox occurred under the constellation Aries. The mysterious character of the Mithraic cult would have arisen from the fact that only the small scientific community would have known about the precession, and an even smaller group, the Stoics of Tarsus, would have interpreted the phenomenon. Viewing themselves as the witnesses to a divine revelation, they would have been select in sharing it with others, and to do so would involve a lengthy process of instruction and initiation.[51]

Ulansey concludes that the appeal of the Mithras cult lay in its ability to claim control of the cosmos and guarantee "astral immortality," the belief set out in Plato's *Timaeus* that human souls become stars upon the death of the body by returning to the celestial sphere whence they came. During the Hellenistic period, this kind of immortality gained great currency.[52]

## Mithraic Interpretation of the Cosmos

The cycles associated with the stars and planets were not without meaning. Both the solar and lunar years, for example, represented a whole pattern of humiliation

---

49. Ibid., 77.

50. Ulansey (ibid., 81) explains that the Stoics of Tarsus would have become familiar with findings of Hipparchus through Posidonius, who lived in Rhodes just after Hipparchus died there.

51. Ibid., 82–84.

52. Ulansey (ibid., 84–87) cites the writings of Apuleius, Heraclides Ponticus, and even Saint Paul and Origen to support this view.

and exaltation, later "Mithraized."[53] Particularly important in the Mithraization was the winter solstice flanked by the seasonal equinoxes.

The sun's journey, as it went from the summer to winter solstices and passed through the autumnal and vernal equinoxes, was seen as a process of a descent to humiliation, with a corresponding assent to exaltation.[54] To read this process, the zodiac was divided into four quadrants paralleling the four seasons. Thus, constellations of summer were Cancer, Leo, and Virgo; of autumn: Libra, Scorpios, and Sagittarius; of winter: Capricorn, Aquarius, and Pisces; and of spring: Aries, Taurus, and Gemini.

From the summer solstice to the autumnal equinox, as daylight began to wane, the ancients saw the exalted sun as moving by increasing degrees from exaltation to humiliation every day. In the spring, the process reversed itself. In the sun's passing through Cancer to Virgo, then, it was seen as exaltation humiliated; from Libra through Sagittarius, humiliation humiliated, with utter debasement happening at the winter solstice; from Capricorn to Pisces, humiliation exalted; from Aries to Gemini, exaltation exalted, with supreme exaltation at the summer solstice.[55]

Such cosmic order had manifold meanings associated with it. Timaeus, we recall, saw the universe as a living creature with a soul. The high point of the sun at the northern hemisphere's summer solstice was considered the "soul gate," through which the sun entered to begin its descent.[56] Likewise, the low point of the sun in the southern hemisphere at the winter solstice stood as the "soul gate" for the sun to pass through as it started to exalt from its humiliation. Hence, in viewing the sun's path, the ancient observer saw a movement from north to south and back again, from high point to low point and back again, from power to weakness and back again, and from heaven to earth and back again.[57]

The lunar year also had its cycles and zodiacal signs, which more or less followed those of the sun. The lunar year is more variable than the solar one, and therefore replacing the equinoxes and solstices are ascending and descending "nodes," the points in which the moon's orbit appears to cross the solar ecliptic in a draconic month.[58] It takes eighteen and one-sixth years for a node to move the 360 degrees of the zodiac.[59] Nonetheless, in the ideal, draconic month, there

---

53. Roger L. Beck, Lecture: "Exaltation/Humiliation: Coding in Word and Image in Mithraism, Ancient Astrology, and Early Christianity" (Toronto, ON: SBL Annual Meeting, Nov. 24, 2002).

54. Ibid.

55. Ibid.

56. Needless to say that these interpretations are from those dwelling in the northern hemisphere.

57. Beck, "Exaltation/Humiliation."

58. A draconic month takes 27.21 days as opposed to a sidereal month of 29.53 days.

59. Beck, "Exaltation/Humiliation."

is the same process of exaltation humiliated, humiliation humiliated, humiliation exalted, and exaltation exalted.[60]

The Mithraization was the astrological interpretation of these astronomical phenomena. Adherents of the Mithraic mysteries took the standard map of the universe, added the soul gates and location of the deities to it, and constructed their mithraea as the model of the universe.[61]

One enters the mithraeum on the autumnal side of the equinox axis. The spring equinox is marked by a cult niche directly opposite the entrance. This axis is considered the equator. Ninety degrees to one's left are the constellations of the summer solstice (Cancer and Gemini), and likewise, ninety degrees to one's right are the constellations of the winter solstice (Sagittarius and Capricorn). The axis running between the two solstices is considered the pole. At the perpendicular junction of the two axes is the seat of Mithras, "at the equinoxes on the equator."[62] The seat of Mithras forms a cross.

The initiate into the Mithraic cult participated in a mimesis of the solar journey. By walking through the four seasons, the candidate imitated earthly life, beginning with mortal death at the winter solstice (humiliation humiliated). He then began the ascent to immortality by passing through the spring equinox on the way to the summer solstice (exaltation exalted).[63] Furthermore, the candidate undertakes this journey beneath the cross of Mithras.

Primarily the sun yet also the moon therefore formed the basis of the cosmic symbol system. Not only did they represent journeys swinging from north to south, but on a metaphorical level, they also shared the life force or soul of the universe, a living creature, and as such they excited the imaginations and philosophies of the people.

---

60. Ibid.

61. Beck (ibid.) quoting Porphyry, *De antro nympharum* 6.24; see, e.g., Mithraeum of the Seven Spheres, in Ostia.

62. Beck, "Exaltation/Humiliation."

63. Beck (ibid.) quoting Porphyry, *De antro nympharum* 6; cf. Mithraeum of the Seven Spheres in Ostia.

## Chapter 2

# The Interplay of Hellenistic and Jewish Thought

Despite the progress in astronomy made by both Greeks and Romans, a common conclusion is that Jewish thought held to the Near Eastern cosmological construct set forth in the OT books and the cultures of the Fertile Crescent. J. Edward Wright opines that such tenacity stems from a desire on the part of the ancient Jews to maintain their cultural heritage in the face of Greco-Roman influences.[1] In addition, the central focus of the Jewish literature is the moral architecture of the universe. Despite the difficulty many had in understanding Greco-Roman cosmology,[2] the basic Jewish assumption was that the interplay of the heavenly bodies had to reflect God's laws for human existence.[3]

Several pseudepigraphic works and even a Pauline epistle challenge this assumption, however.

Wright maintains that the New Testament provides a view of heaven that is not much different from the Jewish one, with the exception of Paul's description in 2 Corinthians, where the writing reflects the Greco-Roman model of multiple heavens:[4]

> I know someone in Christ who, fourteen years ago (whether in the body or out of the body I do not know, God knows), was caught up to the third heaven. And I know that this person (whether in the body or out of the

---

1. J. Edward Wright (*The Early History of Heaven* [New York: Oxford University Press, 2000], 119–23) makes this assessment after studying *1 En.* 1–36. Enoch is a late work of the OT period, yet it perpetuates the Near Eastern cosmology. *1 En.* 58–69 describes a reward for the righteous and punishment for the wicked (esp. *1 En.* 61–63), a point that Wright credits to Hellenistic influence. Indeed, Sheol becomes no longer morally neutral and like Hades becomes the place of terrible suffering for grievous misdeeds (Wright, *Heaven*, 124–25). The Qumran writings, although adopting a Hellenistic notion of multiple heavens, likewise based their astronomy on biblical descriptions (ibid., 129–30). The OT apocryphal literature generally leans toward Hellenistic models but does not adopt them (ibid., 132).

2. Wright, *Early*, 138.

3. Ibid., 128.

4. Wright (ibid, 133–35) concludes that NT works, e.g., Hebrews, James, 1–2 Peter, 1–3 John, and Revelation use the Greek terms οὐρανός and οὐρανοί interchangeably and generally continue to keep to the model present in Judaism: a single heaven where God resides.

body I do not know, God knows) was caught up into Paradise and heard ineffable things, which no one may utter. (2 Cor 12:2–4)

Although Paul may have been more concerned with theological questions than cosmological ones, the vocabulary he uses, with slight variation, approximates a Greco-Roman worldview. Paul mentions the "third heaven" and refers to it as "Paradise." In the Hellenistic model, Paradise is in the seventh heaven. If it appears that Paul is depending on the Persian construct of three heavens, it also appears that, for Paul, the number of heavens is not important. The term "third heaven" is employed solely as a superlative, as the following reference to "Paradise" affirms. Not present, however, is any mention of the Semitic terms "firmament," "the dome of the sky," or "the pillars of the earth." Paul may not use the Hellenistic number *seven* to describe the foray into Paradise, but the vision nonetheless penetrates the heavenly spheres. In this case, while Paul the Jew does not show a digression in usage from the pseudepigraphic and apocryphal writings of the intertestamental epoch, he does show a change from what scholars have perceived as canonical Jewish thought.

## *Pseudepigrapha*

The noncanonical Jewish and Christian literature during the intertestamental period echoes the developments within the Greco-Roman world with regard to cosmology. One reason suggested for the easy reception these religious works gave to Greco-Roman science is that the latter's multiple levels of heaven did not threaten the threefold division of heaven, earth, and netherworld; God remained absolutely other.[5] Since science did not threaten their theology, accuracy in referring to and borrowing from the scientific nomenclature would not have been a concern for the Jewish and Christian writers. It seems, however, that this scientific world fascinated these writers and subtly but not always imperceptibly influenced their theology as well.

It is difficult to determine the degree to which these pseudepigraphic and apocryphal texts permeated the Jewish mind-set in the intertestamental era, or how much of this literature was accessible to Gentiles. Nonetheless, there are sufficient traces within the corpus of these works as well as within the archaeological record to lead one to conclude that Greco-Roman ideas of the cosmos found their way into Jewish and Jewish-Christian belief, even if this Hellenistic cosmology was not at the front and center of that belief.[6] From this point, one can

---

5. Ibid., 139.

6. The archaeological record from the Galilean synagogues at Hammat Tiberias (fourth century CE), Bet Alpha and Sepphoris (sixth century CE), for example, furnish floor mosaics containing the

tentatively conclude that these noncanonical Jewish and Christian writings found
an easy reception among those God-fearing Gentiles who would also have been
sensitive to the scientific cosmogony of the Hellenistic world. In addition, some
Jewish scholars were equally fascinated with and drawn into this cosmogony.

The *Martyrdom and Ascension of Isaiah* is a case in point. This work consists of
two sections, the Martyrdom (*Mart. Asc. Isa.* 1–5) and the Vision (6–11). M. A.
Knibb, the translator of the piece, dates the composition of the first section to the
first century CE.[7] The dating of the second half is disputed. Knibb acknowledges
that Robert H. Charles sees it as a contemporaneous with the first section, owing
to part of it being quoted in Ignatius's *Epistle to the Ephesians* (19:1), but Knibb
himself holds its composition to mid-second century CE.[8] Even following Knibb's
more cautious approach, a work recorded in 150 CE would reflect traditions in
circulation from an earlier period, and so on this basis, a dating of the tradition
to the first century CE, along with the first section, on Martyrdom, would not be
unreasonable. In any case, both these sections provide an example of the seven
spheres of the cosmos:

> After [one thousand] three hundred and thirty-two days the LORD will
> come with his angels and with the hosts of the saints from the seventh
> heaven, with the glory of the seventh heaven, and will drag Beliar, and
> his hosts also, into Gehenna. And he will give rest to the pious whom he
> finds in the body in this world, but *the sun will be ashamed,* and (to) all
> who because of their faith in him have cursed Beliar and his kings. But
> the saints will come with the LORD with their robes which are stored up
> in the seventh heaven above; with the LORD will come those whose spirits
> are clothed, they will descend and be present in the world. (*Mart. Asc. Isa.*
> 4:14–16b).[9]

Wright says of this piece, "Texts such as this suggest that while some early Jews
and Christians knew of the seven-heaven cosmography, they did not understand
it fully."[10] A better conclusion would be that the Jews and Christians melded the
Greco-Roman understanding into their monotheistic belief system. This writing
at least indicates that in the Jewish and Christian world, as with their pagan

---

zodiac, a Babylonian and Persian invention adopted by the Greeks. At Sepphoris the signs of the zodiac
are accompanied by their respective names translated into Hebrew. Although these three constructions
postdate the intertestamental period and thus are unable to support conclusions regarding first-century
practice and belief, they do show that the influence of Hellenistic thought on Jewish culture was
relentless. Josephus describes the outer curtain in the Jerusalem temple as containing the sidereal
constellations but not the signs of the zodiac (*B.J.* 5.212–14).

7. M. A. Knibb, trans., *Martyrdom and Ascension of Isaiah*, in OTP 2:149–50.
8. Ibid., 150.
9. Ibid., 143–176, esp. 162.
10. Wright, *Early*, 159.

contemporaries, the Lord, as a divine being, dwelt in the seventh heaven, while humans occupied the lower stratum of earth.

The Vision (*Mart. Asc. Isa.* 6–11) describes the prophet Isaiah's journey through the seven heavens. From the seventh heaven, Isaiah will see the Lord descend to the world and become incarnate. Isaiah is told that the Lord's passion and death will be concealed even from the heavens, after which the Lord will ascend back to the seventh heaven with the righteous (*Mart. Asc. Isa.* 7:9–9:18).[11]

Here, too, the seven realms of the heavens form the primary architecture for understanding the cosmos, whether or not the interpretation of each sphere correlates with the Greco-Roman framework. Thus, we really cannot conclude that Jews and Christians did not adopt the Hellenistic cosmology because they did not understand it. More likely, the Jews and Christians adopted it but changed it so that stood within the design, power, and majesty of the one God they knew.

But is this the case? Wright believes so and says, "Initial reaction to the presence of such astrological features in these Jewish contexts is typically one of amazement, yet it is under a theology that maintained that their God was nonetheless the ultimate creator and controller of everything in the cosmos. Use of zodiacal themes and images becomes a statement about God's power over even those celestial bodies that other people thought controlled or influenced human fate."[12] Yet, there is evidence to challenge Wright's assessment. Some Jewish and early Christian scholars apparently refer to the stars and heavens without mentioning or intimating God's dominion over them.

Paul's description of the Paradise and the "third heaven" has a quite similar parallel in *2 En.* 8:1–10:6.[13] The longer J recension of *2 Enoch* reads, "And those men took me from there, and they brought me up to the third heaven, and set me down [there]. Then I looked downward, and I saw Paradise. And that place is inconceivably pleasant" (8:1).[14] As with 2 Cor 12:2–4, the third heaven is synonymous with Paradise. In addition, the scene is further complicated in *2 Enoch* by the fact that Enoch looks *downward* to see Paradise when one would expect him to look upward. Further on one reads that "paradise is in between the corruptible and the incorruptible" (8:4). The translator of the text observes that ancient astronomy made the distinction between "*kosmos*, where order prevailed, and *ouranos*, where things were more irregular, . . . where change was possible."[15] In such a construction, the first and second heavens are the regions of change, while

---

11. Early Christian scribes altered the Jewish text of the *Martyrdom of Isaiah*. Consequently, there are several references to Christ where originally there were none. These emendations are immaterial for this study.

12. Wright, *Early*, 179.

13. Wright (ibid., 160) notices the similarity as well.

14. F. I. Andersen, trans., *2 Enoch*, in *OTP* 1:114.

15. Ibid., 116n1.

the fourth through seventh heavens are changeless. The third heaven contains Paradise and is in between the two.[16]

If we apply the understanding of the third heaven in 2 Enoch to Paul's use of the term in 2 Corinthians, we can conclude that Paul is not using the term "third heaven" as a superlative in place of "seventh heaven" inasmuch as he is demonstrating an understanding of Hellenistic cosmology. In other words, Paul employs "third heaven" because he means everything that the phrase intends in the Greco-Roman world.

The third piece from the OT Pseudepigrapha that reflects the broader, literary, and theological context of the intertestamental period is the Treatise of Shem, a writing that dates from the first century BCE.[17] In twelve chapters, this work records the twelve zodiacal signs, beginning with Aries and ending with Pisces.[18] According to James H. Charlesworth, the language is Semitic, but the corrupt nature of the Syriac text makes it difficult to discern whether the original tongue is Hebrew or Aramaic. Textual evidence settles the locale and date of composition to Alexandria circa 20 BCE.[19]

In terms of the relationship of astrology to Jewish and early Christian thought, the Treatise of Shem is theologically significant in that it compromises the lordship of God over the universe. In its chapters we see the arbitrary character of astrological predictions: "Everyone whose name contains a Bēth, a Yūdh, or Kāph will become ill" (2:1). In addition, like all selections from this genre, it attempts to predict the future: "And the Nile will overflow half its (usual) rate" (4:2). Not only does the Treatise of Shem show that astrological speculation was known among the Jews; it also demonstrates their heightened interest in things celestial just before the birth of Christ. Moreover, its dating to the era when the precession of the equinoxes was shifting from Aries to Pisces has this work stand as a witness to the influence of the findings of Hipparchus and to the rise of the cult of Mithras.[20]

It appears, therefore, that the prevailing opinion that Jewish thought did not adopt the Hellenistic cosmology is not entirely correct. Some pseudepigraphic

---

16. Andersen (ibid.) also observes that the Slavonic terms for "change" and "changeless" find their Greek equivalent in 1 Cor 15:53 as φθαρτόν and ἀφθαρσία respectively, and he concludes that in 15:53 Paul switches from concrete to abstract, where the corruptible does not become incorruptible but rather puts on incorruptibility. I would add that Paul's vocabulary indicates that he makes strong allusions to Hellenistic cosmology in that context.

17. J. H. Charlesworth, trans., Treatise of Shem," in OTP 1:474.

18. Charlesworth (ibid., 473) observes the mistake in which a scribe in his haste omitted Aquarius, which is supposed to come before Pisces, the final constellation. A subsequent scribe added Aquarius to the end along with a note alerting the reader to the error.

19. Charlesworth (ibid., 474–75) highlights that Alexandria was renowned for its astrological ideas.

20. Ulansey, Origins, 50–51. Roughly, with the precession, the vernal equinoxes have occurred under Taurus between 4000–2000 BCE; Aries, 2000–1 BCE; Pisces, 1–2100 CE. The vernal equinox will soon shift to Aquarius in approximately 2100.

literature shows instances where Hellenistic vocabulary and nomenclature took hold, as in *1 Enoch* and the *Martyrdom of Isaiah,* even though these works show little appreciation for the meaning behind Hellenistic cosmology. Other pseud-epigraphic literature, on the other hand, such as the *Ascension of Isaiah* and especially the *Treatise of Shem,* give evidence that the Hellenistic descriptions of the heavens led to Hellenistic interpretations of the same. That Saint Paul reflects the Hellenistic understanding of the cosmos as found in *2 Enoch* indicates that Greco-Roman astrology and astronomy found a hearing within the Jewish world during the intertestamental period.

## Paul and the Gospel of Mark

Paul's influence on the early church is unassailable. He himself not only provides references to his own missionary work; the Acts of the Apostles also renders an account of it. His writings speak of the cosmic Christ while demonstrating that humans can participate in the cosmic life that Christ offers his disciples. The Gospel of Mark, as we shall see, features the same themes.

It is highly probable that Paul employs the concepts, language, and claims of Mithraism to fashion his Christology of the cosmic Christ, and that Mark incorporates these Pauline concepts into his Gospel.

Because Christianity has its foundation in biblical Judaism, Judaism formed the matrix of interpretation for the kerygma. This point is visible in all the Gospel accounts with their many references to the prophets as well as in the rest of the NT, especially the Pauline corpus, with their allusions to the patriarchs and matriarchs of the Jewish faith. This OT background functioned as the bedrock upon which Christianity was erected.

### Paul

For the Christian, any discussion of heaven must take into account the res-urrection of the dead. Although the Hellenistic notions of immortality greatly influenced the Jewish understanding of life after death, the Christian proclama-tion went beyond ideas of the soul's immortality by also stating that the human body, in a glorified state, would be raised from the dead. Not only do the Gospels witness to this belief; so do the Pauline texts, which predate the Gospels.

There is evidence of some type of Christian evangelization in Rome before Paul began his missionary activity there. This evangelization reached Rome certainly before 41 CE, for from Acts 18:1–2 we know that Emperor Claudius expelled some Jews from the capital city in that year for reasons associated with the teachings of Christ.[21] Paul himself probably arrived in Rome sometime in or after 61, and his death under Nero had to occur sometime before the emperor's forced suicide in 68.[22] Calculating the span between these two points makes the length of time Paul spent in that city from seven to eight years. Furthermore, there is some scant evidence that both Paul and Mark would have been at least acquainted with each other if not friends. In Rom 16:13, Paul writes, "Greet Rufus, chosen in the Lord, and his mother and mine." It is unknown whether this Rufus is the same one mentioned in Mark 15:21: "They pressed into service a passer-by, Simon, a Cyrenian, who was coming in from the country, the father of Alexander and Rufus, to carry his cross." Similarly, 1 Pet 5:12 mentions a certain "Silvanus," followed by "Mark" in the next verse. That Silvanus (Silas) was a close associate of Paul's, and that his name surfaces alongside "Mark" in 1 Peter gives strength to the argument that Peter and Paul also knew each other if only through their common co-workers, Silvanus and Mark. Nonetheless, Paul's influence on the early church was great, as his letters attest, and he had direct involvement with the church in Rome.

## Summary of Part One

We can return to Wedderburn's four caveats to see how well this study stands under them.

We have discussed how Mithraism provided the religious, scientific, and philosophical vocabulary for the cosmology in Mark. Is there any evidence that Christianity influenced Mithraism? Yes, but not at this early period.[23] The mithraea in the city of Rome, the provenance of Mark's Gospel, postdate the writing of the Gospel by at least fifty to one hundred years. At that time, there is evidence of Christian influence on Mithraism by the fact that followers of Mithras and Christ often met at the same place, but not amicably so.[24] There are also the Pauline and patristic writings against Mithraism, which would not have been written if Christians had not moved back and forth between the two camps.

---

21. See also Suetonius, *Claudius* 25. For an in-depth treatment on the dating of the expulsion of Jews from Rome, see Jerome Murphy-O'Connor, *Paul: A Critical Life* (Oxford: Clarendon Press, 1996), 9–18.

22. The procurator Porcius Festus ruled from 60–62 CE, and according to Acts 25:12, he sends Paul to Rome. See also Josephus, *A. J.* 20.182.

23. Hans Dieter Betz in "The Mithras Inscriptions of Santa Prisca and the New Testament" (*NovT* 10, no. 1 [January 1968]: 65) reports the incantations that a Mithraic liturgical text makes to the elements of creation and concludes that for Paul to castigate Christians for doing the same (Gal 4:3, 8–10; Col 2:8, 20) must mean the Christians were engaged in such a practice.

24. For example, see the Church of Santa Prisca on the Aventine Hill in Rome. A wall separated a mithraeum from a house church in the second century CE, and the mithraeum shows signs of destruction at the hands of the Christians.

This research shows that Paul's theology is not isolated from the Christian heritage. Paul quotes Jewish prophets and responds to Jewish law. He has many references to the Christian Eucharist and reflects the thought of both canonical and deuterocanonical works. His reliance on Mithraic language and interpretation does not negate his dependence on Judaism, which at this time was the basis of the Christian heritage.

We know that insofar as Paul may employ Mithraic concepts and vocabulary, he also reacts against the mystery cults and pagan sects that surrounded him and his society. He takes believers to task for following the "elemental powers of the world" (Gal 4:1–11; Col 2:6–20), and he gives strong advice against eating meat offered to idols (1 Cor 8:1–13) as well as against idol worship in general (1 Cor 10:1–22).

This study does not claim that everything in the Pauline corpus or Mark's Gospel descends from Mithraism. Indeed, far from it. Its assertion is that Paul, in relaying the kerygma, draws from the imagery, iconography, and cultural inheritance of the Mithraic cult championed in his native city of Tarsus, which itself relies on the worldview explicated in Plato's *Timaeus*. Paul uses this Hellenistic worldview as a vehicle to transmit the Christian message, and that message itself arises from a solidly Jewish stalk. The nascent Christian community in Rome for which the evangelist Mark wrote, tied to both the writings and life of Paul, interpreted the kerygma in a Pauline vein but also through the Gospel traditions it had inherited. Mark fashioned the two strains into the Gospel. As a result, the Gospel of Mark proclaims a cosmic Christ.

## Mithraic Context

The *Timaeus* forms the necessary, scientific framework for the Mithraic belief system. It also features a discussion of the creation of the cosmos in which the creatures within the cosmos have corruptible bodies whose purpose is to house the immortal soul. Hellenistic mystery cults support such concepts.

No extant Mithraic texts have been found with which to study, compare, or contrast Jewish and Christian Scriptures. There are only writings about the Mithraic cult and archaeological sites as sources for understanding its worship and belief, and even these Mithraic sites in Rome postdate Mark's Gospel. Nonetheless, because Mithraism contains elements from Plato's *Timaeus*, both Jewish and Gentile inhabitants of the Greco-Roman civilization evidence the thought and vocabulary of its worldview. Paul's association with Tarsus in Cilicia allowed him to "Christianize" Mithraic concepts for the early Christian church, especially the community in Rome.

As David Ulansey shows, Mithraism melded the astronomical findings of the *Timaeus*, enhanced by discovery of the equinoctial precession, with the astrological system of the Stoics. By the first century CE, the worship of Mithras took hold in the eastern regions of the Roman Empire, and it was a cult that claimed control of the cosmos and promised adherents astral immortality by allying themselves with the hero god.

In its reliance on the zodiac and the solar year, Mithraic belief presented the cosmos as running a cycle of exaltation to humiliation and back to exaltation, and according to the *Timaeus*, the cosmos was a living soul. Initiates imitated this journey in the mithraeum.

The Hellenistic worldview and in some cases Hellenistic interpretation surface in Jewish and Christian literature as well, particularly in the pseudepigraphic and apocryphal works. A case in point is the similarity Paul's description of his heavenly vision (2 Cor 12:1–4) has with the portrayal of Paradise in *2 En.* 8:1–10:6.

In his writings Paul relies on a Mithraic vocabulary and symbol system to develop his cosmology. Paul's preaching and teaching in Rome in the years before his martyrdom, when combined with the highly plausible point that Mark and Paul knew each other, influence Markan cosmology. This influence is visible in Mark's treatment of Jesus' baptism, the emphasis on discipleship and the way of the cross, especially in the Bartimaeus pericope, and finally in the original, seemingly open-ended resurrection account written to transmit the awe and wonder of the risen Christ.

Within a century after Mark's Gospel was penned, its cosmological emphasis provided the Roman Christian community, and eventually the whole church, with the ability to counter the claims of Mithras once that cult appeared on the scene in full force.

*Part Two*

# The Gospel of Mark

# Chapter 3

# Markan Themes

That aspects of Greco-Roman cosmology would surface in the Markan Gospel does not suggest that a reader can or should find a one-to-one correspondence between Mithraism and the Markan text. The reader should remember that this study's thesis is that the NT literature, especially the works of Paul and Mark, absorbed the cultural atmosphere, or Zeitgeist. What surfaces in the Markan text is a worldview that reflects a cultural and intellectual system seeking salvation from malicious forces in the cosmos. Deliverance could only come, therefore, from powers that could trump those opposing forces. The most evil and most encompassing force of all malice, naturally, is death. During the intertestamental period adherents of astral religions such as Mithraism were seeking their own immorality.

The most apparent dimension of Mark's cosmological emphasis is seen in Jesus' struggle with Satan, the lord of death, and this fight is enhanced by five ancillary themes. Naturally, Gospel texts are polychromatic, and passages used to describe one theme may also be used to inform another. Nonetheless, the themes of divine communication, divine authority, eschatology, messianic secret, and discipleship all support the account of Jesus' cosmic battle against Satan, and they therefore deserve closer inspection.

The direction of this study shows that Mark's Gospel, written in Rome between 60–70 CE, has religious and philosophical elements within it that employ a cosmology having close affinity with that of Paul. This cosmology uses the language and concepts reflecting awareness and familiarity with a Hellenistic scientific worldview combined with popular Hellenistic interpretations of that worldview. For science, the worldview was framed in Plato's *Timaeus*, and from that understanding developed the religio-philosophical system of Mithraism. Mithraism itself has themes nearly identical to those found in Mark's Gospel. The similarities and differences between the two provide a Markan reading that was well equipped to meet the social and intellectual obstacles of its day as well as providing thought for dealing with the challenges of our own time.

This study now delves into the Gospel of Mark to see how the five aforementioned themes surface in the Markan text. The end result is a composite picture showing the Gospel of Mark as a cosmic battle that Jesus wins at the resurrection, and at that point the eschaton arrives. Disciples of Jesus participate in the same battle, knowing through faith that Christ has already gained the victory. Creation ultimately has communion with the divine, and the Markan writer fashions the kerygma as a proclamation of this divine communication and communion. Afterward, this study will focus on three Markan pericopes that utilize the Greco-Roman worldview of the universe as the means to demonstrate the salvation of that universe: the baptism of Jesus (1:9–11), the healing of Bartimaeus (10:46–52), and the death and resurrection of Jesus (15:33–16:8).

## Divine Communication

In this section, we look at the way the Father communicates his love for his creation.

### Mark 1:9–11, Baptism

A central feature of Mark's Gospel is the bridging of the divide separating earth from the heavens. The baptism of Jesus begins the process (1:9–13). By drawing on some of his prophetic predecessors, John, the last of the OT prophets, places Jesus in a Jewish context. In baptizing Jesus, John connects Jewish prophecy with its fulfillment.[1] The action is written in the passive voice in order to blunt the scandalous fact that the lesser John baptizes and thus legitimizes the greater Jesus. This point is a problem for the other three Gospels as well.

The baptism opens the heavens, thus allowing the Deity to touch creation. Creation's response comes at the death of Jesus, in 15:33–41. Linking these two accounts together is the Greek verb σχίζω, which appears in Mark only at 1:10 and 15:38. At the baptismal passage, the verb σχίζω (pass. ptc.) describes the rending of the heavens (1:10) as it introduces two concomitant actions: the descent of the Spirit and the voice from heaven, "You are my beloved Son; with you I am well pleased" (1:10–11).

The quotation itself comes from at least two OT texts, Ps 2:7 and Isa 42:1–2, with overtones of Davidic sonship and the Suffering Servant respectively. The voice also foreshadows the transfiguration (9:2–10).

### Mark 9:2–10, Transfiguration

After delineating what it means to be a disciple and to pick up the cross, Jesus (albeit only to Peter, James, and John) provides a vision of the final end his followers can expect. The reaction of these disciples now is similar to their reaction

---

1. In at least two places in Mark, John the Baptist is considered a prophet. There is also evidence that the Markan community identified him with Elijah. See 8:28 and 11:32.

at the calming of the storm (4:41) and the walking on the water (6:49–50); they are filled with fear owing to incomprehensible things they have seen before their eyes (9:6). There is an important difference with the transfiguration, however.

Whereas the account of the baptism speaks about the Spirit coming to Jesus as a dove, with a voice from heaven speaking to Jesus, the transfiguration passage describes a cloud overshadowing or covering Jesus, Peter, James, and John. There is also a voice "from the cloud" declaring in the third person Jesus' identity along with a second-person plural imperative: "Listen to him" (Mark 9:7). Any similarity with the baptism is limited to the voice, but even here the parallel is not exact. In the baptism the statement is in the second person, leading to the conclusion that only Jesus heard it; in the transfiguration the voice is speaking to Jesus and the others. They all hear the message. In each case, however, the voice asserts Jesus' divine sonship: in the former, to Jesus alone; in the latter, to Jesus and three disciples. Furthermore, the voice at the baptism at the beginning of the Galilean ministry and the voice here at the start of the journey to Jerusalem point to the centurion's claim at the cross in 15:39.[2]

Jesus' admonition to secrecy "except when the Son of Man had risen from the dead" (9:9) makes the transfiguration a foreshadowing of the resurrection. Indeed, the presence of Moses and Elijah, the former with his mysterious burial (Deut 34:6) and the latter with his ascension (2 Kgs 2:11), augments the eschatological character of the whole transfiguration scene. The appearance of Elijah also prefigures the crucifixion (15:35–36). In this eschatological vein, centered as it is on Jesus' death and resurrection, the transfiguration depicts the glory open to those who follow Jesus through his suffering and death, and shows how one saves one's life by losing it, a process opposed to the ways of Satan and this "generation."[3]

Mark tells us that Peter, James, and John are "terrified" (9:6). Although the term ἔκφοβος means "frightened," the sense is closer to "awestruck." The fact that the three do not run supports this interpretation, and for this reason their reaction prefigures the response of the women at the tomb in 16:1–8.

Jesus utters one final cry before he dies (15:37). The temple curtain then tears from top to bottom (15:38).[4] This verse shows the second and final occurrence of the verb σχίζω, the Greek verb that describes the rending of the heaven at the baptism (1:10). At the baptism the heavens split as God reaches down to creation,

---

2. See John R. Donahue and Daniel J. Harrington, *The Gospel of Mark* (SP 2; Collegeville, MN: Liturgical Press, 2002), for a companion piece in reading the Markan Gospel.

3. As Jesus confirms in 8:12.

4. The temple had a number of curtains associated with it at various periods in history. Specifying exactly to which curtain Mark and the other Synoptic writers are referring is nearly impossible. For further discussion on this matter, see Michael Patella, *The Death of Jesus: The Diabolical Force and the Ministering Angel* (CahRB 43; Paris: J. Gabalda, 1999), 152–57.

and at the death the curtain hiding God's earthly dwelling splits as creation cries to heaven through the crucified Jesus.

The salient point concerning the verb σχίζω is that at both the baptism and the death it describes the tearing open of two supernatural realities, one in heaven and the other in the temple, thus allowing for mutual communication between two realms. The iniative comes from God at the Baptism, and creation responds at the death. Both Ezekiel (1:1) and Isaiah (64:1 [63:19]) speak of the heavens rending at a time of apocalyptic judgment.

## Divine Authority

Jesus must repeatedly prove to the religious establishment that he has authority that transcends theirs, not only as he preaches, cures, heals, and performs miracles, but also as he makes pronouncements that counter their teachings. Mark displays for the reader the origins of Jesus' authority and the way that authority is manifested in his earthly ministry

### Mark 1:1–8, Introduction

The Markan text opens with the stark phrase "The beginning of the gospel of Jesus the Christ [the Son of God]" (1:1). The very first word, Ἀρχή, is freighted with meaning. On its most basic level, it signifies "beginning or first," but on another plane it represents "origin, first cause, earthly or spiritual reigning power, authority, ruler, or elementary principle."[5] Scholars are divided over whether Mark intends the first or second meaning. The context of the whole Markan Gospel, however, favors the second interpretation.

Ἀρχή is employed by the LXX in Gen 1:1 to describe the beginning of all creation under the rule, power, authority, and initiative of God. Using the same vocabulary here in Mark establishes a parallel with Genesis. The gospel is a new creation and also under God's initiative and authority. This reading is substantiated by the phrase "the Son of God."

The inclusion of υἱοῦ θεοῦ is disputed among the textual witnesses. Codices Sinaiticus, Vaticanus, and Bezae all contain the phrase, although in the case of Sinaiticus, it was probably added by the first corrector. Nonetheless, the mention of Ἰησοῦ Χριστοῦ alone keeps the parallel with Genesis. If later copyists added υἱοῦ θεοῦ, they did so to emphasize a point already understood by the community. The phrase also forms part of the triad of sonship titles employed by Mark throughout the Gospel, along with Son of Man and Son of David.

---

5. Matt 24:21; Mark 10:6; 13:19; Luke 20:20; John 1:1–2; 8:25; 1 Cor 15:24; Eph 1:21; Col 1:18; 2:15; and also cf. Acts 3:15; 5:31.

The prophetic quotation in Mark 1:2–3, composed of elements from Exod 23:20; Mal 3:1; and Isa 40:3, ties the OT to John the Baptist's preaching. The Baptist himself ministers in a way similar to other OT prophets, particularly Elijah and Elisha. This reference also gives us a clue into the composition of the Markan community. There would have to be Jewish members within it for whom this quotation would make sense.

In his prophetic statement, John speaks about someone coming after him who will be "mightier" than he. The term used, ἰσχυρός (1:7, with a comparative sense), is also employed at Mark 3:27 where the comparison is such that a strong man represents Satan who is bound by the stronger Jesus. In this sense, ἰσχυρότερός is a key word enabling this introductory section of Mark to foreshadow the events and purpose of Jesus' mission. The mention of the "Spirit" (1:8) represents the power and action of God. It surfaces again at the Beelzebul controversy (3:29) and the apocalyptic discourse (13:11).

## Mark 1:21–28, Expelling Unclean Spirits

The synagogue at Capernaum, featuring both teaching/preaching and demonic expulsion, not only portrays the first actions of Jesus' earthly ministry; it also forms the basis on which to interpret both his preaching on one side, and his healing and expelling unclean spirits on the other.

Jesus enters the Capernaum synagogue and teaches. The people are amazed at his instruction because, unlike the scribes, he teaches with authority (ἐξουσία, 1:22). "Immediately" a person with an unclean spirit cries out and identifies this man teaching with authority as "the Holy One of God" (1:24). Jesus casts out the unclean spirit, and the people ask, "What is this? A new teaching with authority. He commands even the unclean spirits and they obey him" (1:27). Although written as two distinct actions of preaching and exorcising, there is a single interpretation: this person with true teaching authority controls the supernatural world. In fact, the term used, ἐξουσία, also means "supernatural or ruling power."[6] In this sense, Jesus' authority has been established "from the beginning" with ἀρχή (1:1), a term that signifies the origin or first cause of ruling power and authority.

Some religious leaders challenge Jesus' authority when he cures the paralytic in Capernaum (2:1–12). The issue arises when Jesus forgives the man his sins (2:5); if he were simply to cure the paralytic, Jesus would show himself a prophet and nothing more. By offering forgiveness, he takes on God's role. On the other hand, if Jesus were only to pronounce forgiveness, he certainly would be seen as an imposter and nothing more. His twofold action, therefore, proves his "authority"

---

6. Matt 7:29; 9:6, 8; 10:1; 21:23–27; 28:18; Mark 1:22, 27; 2:10; 3:15; 6:7; 11:28–33; Luke 4:6, 32, 36; 5:24; 9:1; 10:19; 12:5; 20:2–8; 22:53; John 1:12; 5:27; 10:18; 17:2; 19:10–11.

as "the Son of Man," a prophetic term in the eyes of the people, "to forgive sins on earth," a divine act (2:10).

### Mark 3:13–19, The Twelve

Jesus shares his authority with the Twelve. Authority is Jesus' to give; he does not pray to the Father to bestow it upon them. Equally important, this authority is "to drive out demons" (3:15), thus meaning a full participation in Jesus' ministry, a participation confirmed when he sends the Twelve out with "authority over unclean spirits" (6:7–13).

### Mark 10:35–45, Authority and Glory

By comparing his authority with the authority of the Gentiles, Jesus extends the conceptual and real distance between the two. Mark indicates that Jesus ventured into pagan territory, thereby claiming those areas for the reign of God as well. To the Jewish religious culture of Palestine, however, the Gentile world, because it did not have the Law, was the area of impurity and false worship. Consequently, Gentile dealings within the social ambit would also reflect a morality antithetical to the ways of God. Since the Gentile world is also under the rule of God, Jesus tells his followers the meaning of this authority: to serve to the point of giving up one's life (10:45).

### Mark 11:27–33, Authority

Jesus refuses to fall into the traps the political and religious powers set for him. If he were to answer plainly that his authority comes from God, he would be liable to charges of blasphemy. These interrogators, however, are not interested in the truth; they only want to intimidate and control, and Jesus knows this fact. By asking the scribes, priests, and elders to answer his question, he is forcing them to declare their intentions. They respond by trying to avoid the predicament and thus concede that Jesus has outsmarted them; hence, Jesus has asserted his authority.

## Eschatology

The prophets as well as John the Baptist and Jesus have spoken of the end times and what they will bring. Drawing on this expectation and literature, Mark presents Jesus as ushering in the eschaton by his ministry.

### Mark 1:14–20, Jesus in Galilee

There are similarities as well as differences between John the Baptist and Jesus. John's ministry is in the area of the Jordan and the district of Jerusalem, while Jesus centers on Galilee. John preaches repentance for the forgiveness of sins; Jesus preaches repentance and belief in the gospel. Jesus' preaching also introduces the fullness of time and the nearness of the kingdom of God (Mark 1:15). There is an eschatological context to the scene. The kingdom of God is the moment in time when all creation will recognize God's original plan and authority. Jesus' ministry then is to hasten this time by conquering those cosmic evil forces — sickness, physical disability, unclean spirits, and death — that have held creation in thrall.

## Mark 13:1–13, Eschatological Discourse

Jesus replies to the disciples' exclamation on the temple's beauty by foretelling the edifice's destruction, and then he leaves the temple precincts, never to return. The rest of the chapter contains the Markan apocalypse (13:3–37). With imagery drawn from canonical, deuterocanonical, and unknown sources, Mark weaves a theological tapestry that forms the interpretive matrix for the upcoming passion, death, and resurrection.

The Mount of Olives, the setting for this discourse, lends it the atmosphere of divine judgment. The Lord fights for Jerusalem from that promontory. In addition, the glory of the Lord flees to it from the temple.[7] The unspecified battles, famines, and insurrections indicate a time of tremendous upheaval. The betrayal of family members probably relates a persecution of the primitive church when such actions were actual occurrences.

## Mark 13:14–23, The Temple

The desolating abomination ushering in the great tribulation can refer to any purity violation of the temple cult, the supreme example of course being a pagan standing within the holy of holies. In point of fact, at the Roman takeover of Palestine in 66 BCE, the general Pompey entered the sanctuary of the Jerusalem temple and surveyed the holy of holies.[8] This event could be Mark's reference, for as far as the historical record indicates, Pompey's move stands as the most recent violation of the temple at the time of Mark's writing.[9] The mention of the "desolating abomination" could also be a *vaticinium ex eventu*, a statement after the fact presented as a prediction of the actual event. In this case, the reference would be to the Roman destruction of the temple in 70 CE, a reading supported by the parenthetical remark in verse 14.[10] Because this apocalyptic account is such an amalgam of sources, it is nearly impossible to establish the referents with any real accuracy.

---

7. Zech 14:1–10ff.; Ezek 11:22–25; 43:1–5; and also 10:18–20.
8. Josephus, *A.J.* 14.72.
9. But see Dan 11:31; 12:11; 1 Macc 1:54; 2 Macc 6:2.
10. If this description is a *vaticinium ex eventu*, it helps in the dating of the Markan Gospel.

## Mark 13:24–27, Son of Man

Jesus applies the phrase "Son of Man" to himself. The quotation here comes from the book of Daniel (7:13–14). The last previous reference to the "Son of Man" comes at Mark 10:45, just before the Bartimaeus pericope (10:46–52). It continues through the rest of the passion as Jesus' self-referential appellation.[11] As others have observed, the "Son of Man" title falls into three categories. The first contains references to Jesus' passion, death, and resurrection (Mark 8:31; 9:9, 12, 31; 10:33–34, 45). The second category is based on its use in the book of Ezekiel (Mark 2:10, 28; 14:21, 41), where the phrase is self-referential and is used in place of a personal pronoun. The third example is from the book of Daniel, which we see here. It too is self-referential, but because Mark draws from the eschatological discourse in Daniel, Jesus' answer to the high priest in 14:62 takes on the Danielic understanding of the phrase, "Son of Man" and links it with Jesus' passion, death, and resurrection. In Daniel 7:13, the "Ancient One" gives the "son of man" "everlasting dominion" over every people and nation and thus the "son of man" receives a divine status. The high priest's reaction to Jesus' declaration in 14:62 shows that he understands Jesus' reference all too well.

## Mark 13:28–36, Conclusion of the Eschatological Discourse

The disciples are admonished to read the signs of the times. The lesson of the fig tree recalls Jesus' curse upon entering Jerusalem (11:12–14). These verses enjoin the disciples to interpret what they see, a warning that gains importance by the fact that no one except the Father knows the day or hour. Moreover, the final moment will come unexpectedly. The cosmic character of these words surfaces at the remark about the passing of heaven and earth. Heaven or the heavens exist beyond and above the earth and planets and are absolutely inaccessible to human beings. With these words, Jesus shows his divine origin. Furthermore, since it is set before the passion narrative within the Markan framework, it establishes the eschatological character of Jesus' death and resurrection.

## Mark 16:1–8, Resurrection

The women's reaction to Jesus' resurrection, specifically their "trembling and bewilderment," notifies the reader that the eschaton has come.[12]

---

11. Mark 14:21, 41, 62.
12. This point receives greater treatment below.

# Messianic Secret

Through much of Mark's Gospel, Jesus stresses silence about himself, a detail that many have called the "messianic secret."[13] Jesus actually explains the "messianic secret" to his followers in Mark 4:10–12.

## Mark 4:10–12, On Parables

The key to the "messianic secret," however, lies in Jesus' explanation on the use of parables.[14] Those who are searching for the kingdom of God will find it in Jesus' ministry and preaching. The secret is also linked to the "mystery" in Mark 4:11. The "mystery" is the revelation of the kind of Messiah Jesus is, the suffering Messiah who is declared to be the "God's Son" in 15:39.[15] On this basis, the titles associated with Jesus become important.

Mark opens the Gospel with a reference to Jesus as the Messiah (and the Son of God; 1:1), a verse that is the source of some textual problems. The title "Son of God" is uttered only three more times in Mark, twice by demons (3:11; 5:7) and once by the Roman centurion at the cross (15:39).[16] Two other "son" titles, "Son of Man" and "Son of David," also appear in Mark's Gospel, and with the Roman centurion's declaration they are fused into "Son of God."

In Mark's Gospel, the appellation "son of David" occurs only three times in two separate pericopes, 10:47–48 and 12:35–37.[17] In both cases, the references are to the greatness of King David. In Jesus' discourse on the meaning of the title (12:35–37), he maintains that in his relationship to David he is in no way subservient to the Jewish king. Nonetheless, both instances evidence that, in terms of the "messianic secret," there was among a major part of the population an expectation that the Messiah, no matter how they conceived the Messiah to be, would be from the house of David, and therefore the Messiah's greatness would come from this royal lineage.

The title "son of man" is used in the OT prophetic tradition, mostly in Ezekiel, where it is nearly always vocative and refers to the prophet himself. It is also found in the apocalyptic passage in Daniel (7:13). When in Mark the title relates to the works and authority of Jesus, it is self-referential. In four passages (2:10, 28; and 14:21, 41), Mark echoes Ezekiel. The other references are to Jesus' passion, death, and resurrection.[18] The title also appears twice in the book of Daniel.[19] The most

---

13. But see 5:19–20.
14. See also 1:25, 34, 44; 3:12; 4:10–11, 34; 5:43; 6:31; 7:24; 9:9, 28, 30; 13:3.
15. See also Donahue and Harrington, *Mark*, 28–29.
16. In Mark 1:24 the unclean spirit calls Jesus "the Holy One of God!"
17. These passages are taken up in detail below.
18. Mark 8:31; 9:9, 12, 31; 10:33–34, 45.
19. Dan 7:13; 8:17.

important of these occurrences is the apocalyptic reference in Dan 7:13, to which Jesus makes a direct allusion in his eschatological discourse (Mark 13:26) and at his trial (14:62). In fact, his use of the title at his trial is the evidence that the leaders use to condemn him (14:63–64).

One discovers the "messianic secret" when one has enough faith to enter into the "mystery of the kingdom of God" (4:11) as a disciple. Jesus' followers have that faith, and that is why the "mystery" has been granted to them, but even they must have the parable of the sower explained to them (4:10–20).

Seeing all the events, the centurion confirms the significance of Jesus' cry by declaring, "Truly this man was God's Son!" (15:39 NRSV). With his statement, the Markan Gospel has reached its climax: the Son of Man,[20] who is also the Son of David,[21] is now confessed by a living person as the Son of God.[22] The centurion is the only human being in Mark's Gospel to acknowledge Jesus' divinity with this title. He has been granted the "mystery of the kingdom of God" because he has "heard the word" through observing Jesus' passion and death, and he has accepted all these things. He is the "rich soil" on which the "mystery of the kingdom of God" will bear "fruit thirty and sixty and a hundredfold" (4:20).

# Discipleship

In the Markan narrative, Jesus preaches, heals, and expels unclean spirits as a band of followers witness his teaching and ministry. Discipleship is an important element in Mark's Gospel. The proper response to Jesus' ministry is to follow him all the way to the cross.

## Mark 8:31–35, First Passion Prediction

Not until the first passion prediction does Jesus make known to his followers the cost of their discipleship; their reaction, voiced by Peter, is negative (8:31–35). Jesus goes beyond correcting Peter in his perceptions; by calling him "Satan," Jesus informs every listener that discipleship without suffering is not discipleship at all. In fact, such an attitude is contrary to the kingdom.

## Mark 9:31–32, Second Passion Prediction

The setting for the second passion prediction is intentionally formal: Jesus is teaching his disciples when he informs them of his upcoming passion, death, and resurrection (9:31). They do not understand what he is saying, and doubtless with the memory of his response to Peter at the first prediction (8:31–35), they

20. Mark 2:10, 28; 8:31, 38; 9:9, 12, 31; 10:33, 45; 13:26; 14:21, 41; 14:62.
21. Mark 10:47–48; 12:35.
22. Mark 1:1; 3:11; 5:7; 15:39.

are afraid to ask any questions and so remain silent (9:32). On a broader level, their fear and silence stem from their reluctance to enter into the mystery of the kingdom of God (4:11) and thus are linked to the "messianic secret."

## Mark 10:32–34, Third Passion Prediction

At the third passion prediction the disciples also display both fear and mis-understanding. As they are making their way to Jerusalem, Mark reports that the disciples are "amazed" and followers are "afraid" (10:32). Jesus senses their emotional state but separates out the Twelve from the rest of the followers. He continues by giving more detail of what lies ahead. As with Peter at the first prediction and the other group at the second prediction (9:31–32), the sons of Zebedee remain clueless on what following Jesus means (10:35–38).

In his explanation, Jesus speaks about "the baptism with which I am baptized" and how the two will undergo it as well (10:38–39). At Jesus' own baptism, the Spirit "like a dove" was descending upon him as he himself was coming up from the Jordan, and there is the voice from the heavens: "You are my beloved Son; with you I am well pleased" (1:9–11). In this passion prediction scene, does Jesus mean that James and John will have a similar experience, or rather does Mark mean that those entering the community can expect the same?

We know from the archaeological and written record that baptism was a part of Christianity almost from the very beginning.[23] It was and is the process by which someone becomes a disciple, a member of the community. At Jesus' baptism, one word is of interest, ἀναβαίνω, when Jesus comes up from the water. We can assume that if Jesus "comes up" at the end, he would have "gone down" (καταβαίνω) at the beginning. Hence, we have a double action of descent and ascent.[24] This twofold action of descent and ascent becomes the interpretive key for discipleship into the "mystery of the kingdom of God" or "messianic secret" (4:11). As we will see in the major Markan theme of the cosmic battle, Jesus' major weapon, humiliation, leads to his victory, exaltation. Discipleship becomes a constitutive part of the cosmic battle, and Mark connects discipleship with baptism through the healing of blind Bartimaeus (10:46–52), the passing reference to a naked young man (14:51–52), and the presence of the young man at the tomb (16:5). The alacrity with which Bartimaeus, the last disciple of Jesus' earthly ministry, follows Jesus to Jerusalem makes him a model for all.

---

23. Etienne Nodet and Justin Taylor, *The Origins of Christianity: An Exploration* (Collegeville, MN: Liturgical Press, 1998), 57–88.

24. Mark may be fashioning a wordplay here with the term καταβαίνω, used to describe the Spirit's descent in 1:10.

## Cosmic Battle

The cosmic battle forms the greatest part of the Markan Gospel. It encompasses the whole earthly ministry up to and including the passion, death, and resurrection. The five themes above are subsumed under this central focus.

### Mark 1:12–13, Temptation in the Desert

The desert, a place of extreme testing on a natural level, now becomes the scene of supernatural testing as well. Mark stresses the urgency of Jesus' mission with the adverb "immediately" (εὐθύς) in 1:12.[25] The text reads that the Spirit "casts" or "expels" Jesus into the desert (ἐκβάλλω). This violent action is singular to Mark and undergirds Jesus' priority of action. The redemption of the cosmos begins with facing the enemy head to head and toe to toe. Angels minister to Jesus, although the content of this ministry is not clear. As heavenly messengers, the angels at least provide the divine presence in a moment of trial.

### Mark 1:16–20, Call of Disciples

The number and names of the first disciples are difficult to fix. Matthew's version (4:18–22) follows Mark's. Luke (6:12–16), however, does not mention Thaddeus and has Simon the Zealot as opposed to Simon the Cananean. Similar complications arise in the remaining call narratives.[26] Jesus prepares to set out on his ministry. As with any commander, he must have an army, and he must teach his followers the identity of the real foe while instructing them on methods of fighting.

### Mark 1:21–2:12, Expelling and Healing, a Microcosm

With the expulsion of the demon from the "man with an unclean spirit" as the first example, we can say that Jesus' ministry falls into three, often overlapping, categories that can be delineated as cleansing of demons, healings either from illness or physical abnormality, and preaching. The first two categories are so close that it is better to speak of their interconnectedness rather than their division. A good example of the entwined relationship arises in the first deeds of Jesus' ministry (Mark 1:21–45).

When his followers find Jesus praying in a deserted spot (1:35–39), Simon informs him that everyone is looking for him. Jesus answers by saying that he must go to "preach" in the nearby villages. He identifies preaching as the very purpose of his mission (1:38), and the account, using two present active participles,

---

25. Mark uses εὐθύς nearly 40 times within the Gospel, compared to seven instances for Matthew and one for Luke. Author's translation.

26. See also John 1:35–51.

κηρύσσω and ἐκβάλλω, states that Jesus went into their synagogues and the whole of Galilee, driving out demons and preaching. No description of any expulsion follows at this point, however. Indeed, the next two pericopes, the cleansing of a leper (1:40–45) and the healing of the paralytic (2:1–12), relate two cures. In the latter, Jesus addresses the paralytic, and the scribes ask, "Why does this man speak that way? He is blaspheming. Who but God alone can forgive sins?" (2:7). That the scribes utter it here foreshadows one of the accusations leveled against Jesus, and this charge of blasphemy surfaces again at the trial by the Sanhedrin in 14:64.

Thus, Jesus' initial actions consist of driving out demons (1:21–28), several healings (1:29–34), preaching (1:35–39), and another two healings (1:40–45; 2:1–12). The preaching (1:35–39) provides the interpretation for these healings and demon expulsions. The attention that Jesus pays to the possessed, the sick, and the lame presents a microcosm of the cosmic battle. The battle with the forces of evil is fought in the daily suffering and trials of people. By attending to these needs, Jesus wages war on Satan.

## Mark 2:13–22, Levi

The next scene, the call of Levi, is similar to the previous call of disciples (1:16–20). The minute Jesus calls him, Levi rises and follows. Being a tax collector, however, makes him a sinner, as the subsequent dinner conversation demonstrates. The same questions on ritual purity continue into the next scene, when the two groups of disciples, those of John the Baptist and those of the Pharisees, question Jesus' followers about their master's lack of attention to ritual purity. Jesus responds with the parable of the old and new wineskins (2:18–22).

## Mark 2:23–28, Sabbath

The controversies sparked by Jesus and his small band increase when they pluck grain while walking through the field on the Sabbath. The resolution comes when Jesus proclaims his lordship over the Sabbath; in so doing, he claims equality with the God of Sinai, the creator of the world and the law (2:27–28). The curing of the person with the withered hand, the next passage, confirms this point.

## Mark 3:1–6, Synagogue

For the second time in the Markan account, Jesus enters a synagogue on the Sabbath. The first time he did so (1:21–28), he began to teach. This second instance says nothing about Jesus teaching in the synagogue. Nonetheless, in this period the synagogue was a place of Scripture reading, preaching, and teaching. In addition, Jesus must have been located in some position that commanded the attention of the assembly, for the Pharisees were watching him to see if he would cure anyone (3:2). We only hear of Jesus speaking to the one with the withered hand and to the Pharisees (3:3–4). Jesus does cure the individual but first intimates that such authority is his (3:4). In his explanation, he reminds the crowd that everything good and life-giving belongs to the Sabbath; by extension, whatever is evil and death-dealing does not (3:4). At this point his enemies leave the synagogue to plot on how to kill him, thus allying themselves with the powers of death (3:6). Once again, healing is used as an occasion for instruction.

## Mark 3:7–12, Gentiles

In this pericope, it is not as obvious as in previous examples whether Jesus is preaching. The text says that crowds also come from the pagan districts of Idumea, from beyond the Jordan, as well as from Tyre and Sidon, and they come to Galilee because they hear what he is "doing" (3:8). In the previous passages, in entering synagogues and dining with Pharisees, Jesus has been in a totally Jewish environment. To speak about the Law and the Prophets is a perfectly understandable way for him to gain a hearing and to assert his authority among Jews, but the Law is of no importance to those in far-flung pagan territories. Rather than coupling preaching with healing in this scene, Mark highlights healing and expelling demons. Those with various diseases press upon Jesus, and they are cured. Simultaneously, at the mere sight of Jesus, the unclean spirits are immediately intimidated. As with the man in the synagogue (1:23–24), they are the only ones who recognize his true identity as "the Son of God" (3:11).[27]

## Mark 3:13–19, The Twelve

The explicit connection of preaching with expulsion resurfaces as Jesus chooses the Twelve. Jesus selects them so that they would preach and have the authority to cast out demons, to share fully in his ministry. Thus far we have seen a steady movement of the preaching/teaching and healing/expelling within Jesus' ministry. The mission begins in relative obscurity at the baptism and temptation (1:9–13) and now is at the point where Jesus' actions have gained him so much publicity that he chooses the Twelve to share in it. At this point, Jesus has the greatest debate yet with the scribes, the outcome of which defines the very purpose, character, and truth of his mission.

## Mark 3:20–30, Beelzebul Controversy

With Jesus' own family thinking that he is out of his mind, the Jerusalem scribes take the opportunity to accuse him of complicity with Beelzebul (3:20–22). For them, anything or anyone that manifests elements of the supernatural cannot be

27. In Mark 1:23–24 an unclean spirit specifically calls Jesus "the Holy One of God!"

from God; it can only be from the prince of demons. Thus, in a total rejection of the good that Jesus has taught and done, they assign the preaching, healing, and expelling demons to evil intention and deed. Jesus does not let this assessment go unchallenged. The strength of this parable, however, as well as the following one lies in the borderlines it traces.

Beelzebul and Satan are one and the same enemy.[28] Jesus minces no words; this enemy is his single opposition. Jesus explains the battle in which he is engaged by using the image of the strong man. The story line in the parable of the strong man is transparent. Certainly, if someone is going to rob a house, he has to make sure that the owner will not overpower him in the endeavor. The application to life is made by analogy. In the Markan context, the strong man is Satan, and his house is creation and creatures. Satan, the strong man, has held both creation and creatures captive. Jesus, the one stronger (cf. 1:7), has now arrived on the scene, first to bind Satan and then to reclaim all creation from his clutches. This reclamation stands as the purpose of his whole ministry. Only in this framework does the statement about the sin against the Holy Spirit make sense. The blasphemy of the Jerusalem scribes cannot be forgiven because, by holding Jesus to be an agent of Satan, they reject the very forgiveness offered them. The scene closes with the second reference to Jesus' natural family, which has already expressed its lack of understanding regarding his mission (3:21).

## Mark 3:31–35, True Family

In this section the family still does not acknowledge the scope of Jesus' ministry. To the ear of the listeners, Jesus' statement that family ties rest on one's desire to do "the will of God" is nothing short of revolutionary. In a society where blood kinship and extended families are the basis of one's identity, to claim otherwise indicates both the radical nature and the price of discipleship.

## Mark 4:1–20, Sower and the Seed

There are parallels to the parable of the Sower and the Seed in the other Synoptic accounts, Matt 13:1–9 and Luke 8:4–8. Its position in the Markan narrative, however, provides a miniature description of Jesus' ministry thus far; despite the fact that the parable is not a complicated story, it also features an explanation (Mark 4:13–20).

Satan is the first force of opposition the sown word confronts (4:15). Unlike the other seed that falls along the rocky ground, thorns, and rich soil, respectively, the seed upon the path has no opportunity to germinate and put forth shoots before

---

28. Patella (*Death*, 48–56). By the intertestamental period, the terms "devil," "Beelzebul," and "Satan," although vocabulary representing three different cultural and religious traditions, had become fused into one evil being.

Satan carries the word away. The lesson is that, unless Satan is neutralized, the word never sprouts within the people for whom it is intended, and we have seen this lesson in the ministry up to this point. Jesus proves his mastery over the demonic forces during his temptation in the desert (1:12–13). His first miracle occurs while he is preaching in the Capernaum synagogue, where he drives out the unclean spirit from the person in the assembly who obstructs his teaching (1:21–26). With the unclean spirit gone, the previously possessed is now able to hear Jesus' word. After curing Simon's mother-in-law, he expels demons and prohibits them from speaking, thereby ensuring that his word takes root (1:34). In the very center of Galilean Jewish teaching and preaching, the synagogues, Jesus drives out the demons as he preaches (1:39). For their part, the unclean spirits recognize Jesus' authority and submit to him (3:11–12). The Beelzebul controversy, as we have seen, is a clear example of Satan's hold on the world and his attempts to block its redemption. When the Jerusalem scribes credit Beelzebul with the actions and preaching of Jesus, they deny any hope of the word's efficacy (3:20–22). This theme, by now well established in the Markan narrative, continues throughout the Gospel. Moreover, the next three parables confirm it.

The agricultural metaphor deviates to one involving the light and the bushel, but the lesson is still the same (4:21–23). For those who see that the light is from God, they cannot hide from others, and others cannot hide it from them; the light can only increase. The return to the farming image makes the lesson of the light parable clearer.

## Mark 4:26–34, Parables

Jesus explicitly compares the kingdom of God to the seeds in the next two passages. In the first pericope, we see the goodness that the seed can produce once the hold of Satan has been broken, and the key word in this understanding is γῆς, a word whose primary meaning is "earth, land, ground, soil." In the parables of the Sower and the Seed (4:5, 8), its explanation (4:20), the Growing Seed (4:26, 28), and the Mustard Seed (4:31), γῆς always has a positive meaning. The seed/word always has a good reception on the earth or soil. Wherever the seed does not sprout or the shoot does not last, it is because there is no depth to the soil or the soil is too poor. Satan carries off the seed falling on the path, not seed on the good soil (4:15). Likewise, the Growing Seed yields its grain from the γῆς (4:26), as does the Mustard Seed (4:31).

Such use of γῆς has implications for the whole Markan text. Because the term signifies "earth," it represents not only the path, rocky ground, and the thorns of the parable, but it also incorporates material creation as experienced in the lives of the listeners. In order then for the word to grow and increase, the whole earth and everything in it must be free of Satan's yoke.

## Mark 4:35–41, Calming of the Storm

Jesus' reclamation of creation moves from land to sea in the pericope Calming of the Storm (4:35–41). Because within the biblical tradition, the sea most often represents chaos,[29] and therefore the very opposite of the created order,[30] Jesus' power over the water serves as another manifestation of his lordship over the evil forces. In addition, it also demonstrates his power over nature. This twofold display of power shocks the disciples, and they react in fear. At first they are terrified of drowning and elicit help from Jesus (4:38), but when he does more than they had expected, they remain terrified. Mark shows the degree of their fear by the verbal phrase ἐφοβήθησαν φόβον μέγαν literally, "they feared a great fear," a phrase reflecting a Hebrew/Aramaic infinitive absolute, and thus an intensifier. Their question at the end of the pericope, "Who then is this whom even the wind and sea obey?" (4:41), demonstrates that they themselves still do not know what the demons have long recognized: Jesus is the Son of God; yet, they are awestruck.[31]

## Mark 5:1–20, Gerasene Demoniac

Now that Jesus has already shown his power over nature, evil, and chaos, he lands in pagan territory on the eastern side of the Sea of Galilee, the area named for the "Gerasenes." As the textual tradition shows, this particular locale is difficult to specify. The alternative names of the spot surfacing among all three Synoptics reflect confusion between the cities of Gadara and Jerash. Both these ancient towns, however, were situated in the jurisdiction called the "Decapolis," a group of nominally ten cities yet sometimes numbering as few as seven and as many as eighteen. They were considered solidly pagan areas despite the good number of Hellenized Jews who lived within them. In the Markan account, this is Jesus' first visit to a non-Jewish area, and as such, it broadens the aim of his mission.[32]

   Mark places a great deal of emphasis on the absolutely uncontrollable character of this unclean spirit. Unlike those others with unclean spirits the reader has encountered so far, the person possessed here lives outside the inhabited areas

---

29. See especially Gen 1:1–10, esp. 7–9; Exod 14:9–31; 15:1–21; Pss 33:7; 65:7 [8]; 66:6; 68:22 [23]; 69:15; 74:13; 77:19 [20]; 78:13; 78:53; 89:9 [10], 25 [26]; 93:4; 104:25; 106:9; 114:3–5; 136:6; 146:6; Job 7:12; 9:8; 26:12; 28:14; 38:8, 16; 41:31 [23]; Wis 5:22; 10:18; Sir 24:29; 29:18 [17]; 43:24; Mic 7:19; Jonah 1:1–15; 2:3 [4]; Nah 3:8; Hab 1:14; 3:8; Isa 5:30; 10:26; 17:12; 23:11; 51:10, 15; Jer 5:22; 6:23; 31:35; 50:42; 51:42; Ezek 26:3; 27:26, 34; 28:8; 32:2; Dan 7:2.

30. Gen 1:1–2:3.

31. Mark 1:24, 34; 3:11.

32. Unlike Mark 3:7–12, where Gentiles come to Jesus.

(5:3), and no one can restrain his violent behavior (5:4); the demoniac is nearly feral (5:5). Yet here too, the spirits not only recognize Jesus as the as the Son of God; they also acknowledge his ultimate authority (5:7–10, 12).

It may seem odd that Jesus grants the spirits' request to remain in the district, but he does so by sending them into a herd of swine, animals that according to Jewish tradition are outside the dietary codes and therefore outside Jewish society.[33] When the unclean herd plunges into the sea, the very reality of chaos and evil, Jesus is cleansing this whole pagan district in order to bring it into the kingdom. As the inhabitants discover what has happened, they become fearful of Jesus and beg him to depart; a new creation threatens the old order, no matter how bad the old order is (5:14–17). Yet, the whole world is to be rescued from Satan, and the former demoniac becomes Jesus' agent in preaching as much (5:18–20).

## Mark 5:21–43, Jairus's Daughter and the Hemorrhaging Woman

After Jesus' great exorcism in the pagan Decapolis, he returns to Jewish territory, where he performs two miracles: curing a woman of a hemorrhage and raising a girl from the dead. To portray these deeds, Mark employs an intercalation technique: he surrounds one story within two halves of another. Both passages mutually inform each other. Up until this point, Jesus has initiated all the healings and exorcisms. Here the afflicted take an active role, Jairus for his incapacitated daughter and the woman on her own behalf. Much of the interpretation of this intercalation stands on the interplay of two verbs, σῴζω and ἰάομαι. Whereas ἰάομαι means to "heal," σῴζω is the more comprehensive term and represents to "save," or "rescue." Both Jairus and the hemorrhaging woman seek deliverance. In each case, the verb employed describing their respective requests is σῴζω (5:23, 28).

In a comparison of the two stories, we see Jairus on his knees, beseeching Jesus to save his dying daughter (5:23). Jesus eventually arrives at the synagogue leader's home, only to find the daughter apparently dead. Jesus calms Jairus by telling him to have faith alone (5:36), which he apparently does, and his daughter is brought back to life (5:41–43). With the hemorrhaging woman, on the other hand, there is a twofold process. She had gone to doctors (ἰατρός), but none of them could help her (5:26). She wants more than to be healed of her affliction, however; now she wants to be wholly made well (5:28).

Mark tells us that after touching Jesus' clothes, she is healed (5:29; ἰάομαι). Yet, the story does not end at this point. Jesus' reaction in verse 30 shows that his mission is more than healing people as some miracle worker might. He seeks the identity of the one who touched him because he wants the person who was healed

---

33. See Lev 11:6; Deut 14:7.

to express exactly what she was expecting. In the end, her faith saves her and she is healed (5:34; σῴζω). The story of Jairus's daughter and the hemorrhaging woman, situated immediately after the Calming of the Storm and the Cleansing of the Gerasene Demoniac, place death and physical infirmity within the context of unredeemed creation. In these two examples, Jesus saves humans from the world of suffering and death, an environment that cannot be disentangled from the demonic world of Satan.

## Mark 6:1–13, Rejection at Nazareth and Mission

Jesus' reception at Nazareth stands in sharp contrast to the preceding material on Jairus and the hemorrhaging woman. In those cases, the two had faith in Jesus, and consequently he was able to work wonders. Because of the people's lack of faith, Jesus is not able to do many miracles in Nazareth except curing some people by laying on of hands (6:5). The mission of the Twelve follows the rejection at Nazareth, and the fact that they are able to cure and expel demons makes this pericope stand in contrast to the events at Nazareth.

Jesus gives the Twelve "authority" over the unclean spirits (6:7). This ἐξουσία, as demonstrated from the very beginning of Mark's Gospel, is Jesus' to give (1:22), and they preach, heal, and exorcise exactly as Jesus has done (6:12–13). In terms of the battle Jesus has been waging, he now has followers participating in the battle with him. More personal and dedicated than allies, these followers, as represented by the Twelve, will only be effective if they maintain their faith in him. This issue of faith and desire has surfaced in previous passages in Mark (3:28–30; 5:21–43), and its position here, particularly after a passage showing what happens when there is little faith, underlines its importance.

## Mark 6:14–44, John's Death and Multiplying of Loaves and Fish

Again, Mark uses the intercalation technique. The Twelve are on their mission of preaching, curing, and exorcising. The account of John the Baptist follows (6:14–29), and then the narrative returns to the Twelve and their mission (6:30–31).

Herod hears of Jesus' reputation and immediately concludes that John the Baptist has been raised from the dead. Inasmuch as Mark presents Jesus in a cosmic struggle with Satan, Herod's execution of John is tied to diabolical forces. The strength of its connection with the cosmic battle, however, comes within the subtlety of the passage. In the forces of Satan, death is the ultimate weapon. Herod's misidentification of Jesus with John serves to foreshadow Jesus' own death at the hands of the powerful. That the Baptist's disciples come to claim John's body foreshadows the role of Jesus' disciples at his death.

The attention switches back to the apostles at verse 30. They tell the success of their mission, and Jesus' response is to withdraw with them to a deserted place

(6:31). The setting is important. Up until this point, only Jesus has gone into the deserted places (1:12, 35, 45). In the first instance, he is tempted by Satan, and in the second, he goes off to pray, and in the third he tries to sequester himself from the crowd. Now, the apostles go with him to rest. During their retreat, the size and tenacity of the pursuing crowds necessitate that they feed them, and thus we come to the feeding of the five thousand (6:31–44).

The setting of this miracle in the deserted regions recalls Jesus' own temptation in the desert immediately after his baptism (1:12–13). There, the spirit drives Jesus into the desert, and though tested, Jesus wins over Satan. With the apostles here, however, Jesus invites them into the desert (6:31), and there he abundantly feeds them as well as others, and he does so in what, as far as the Markan narrative is concerned, is Satan's abode.

The mission of the apostles, the death of John the Baptist, and the miraculous feeding are all of a piece that incorporates Jesus' followers more fully into his mission while showing them the price they may all have to pay to be his followers. Simultaneously, Jesus' action in the deserted place makes a claim that the desert, the former dwelling place of Satan, now belongs to Jesus.

## Mark 6:45–52, Walking on the Sea

Similar to the calming of the storm (4:35–41), Jesus' walking on the sea occurs when the disciples are in a boat during a strong wind and high waves (6:48). The symbolic value of his action is similar to the calming of the storm as well. The chaos, which is the water, cannot claim Jesus. Moreover, the biblical tradition indicates that by walking atop the water, Jesus exhibits his lordship over all creation.[34] The reaction of the disciples is noteworthy. They are first "terrified" (6:50), then "astounded" (6:51),[35] and finally Mark says their hearts were made stubborn. The evangelist is emphasizing the point that the disciples are flummoxed and confused about Jesus' identity, despite everything he does to show that he is the Messiah.

## Mark 6:53–56, Curing of the Sick

The pattern continues. Jesus has just exhibited his power over chaos and evil, and now he takes that power to the sick and infirm. His authority reaches in all directions. The mention of touching the tassel of Jesus' cloak indicates the

---

34. The phrase "under his feet" in the LXX and NT, always constructed with either preposition ὑπό or ὑποκάτω and with or without the verb ὑποτάσσω, is nearly always used as an expression of subjection with "enemies," "all things," or "everything" set as the object of the verb (1 Kgs 5:3 [17]; 1 Cor 15:25, 27; Heb 2:8). In the instances where the emphasis is not on the crushed enemies, the predicate is either a "dark cloud(s)," or sapphire tilework — in either case, elements of divine glory (Exod 24:10; 2 Sam 22:10; Ps 18:9 [17:10 LXX].
35. The Greek verb used is ἐξίστημι.

importance of this article of clothing in the ancient world. The hemorrhaging woman in 5:27–28 does exactly the same thing.

## Mark 7:1–23, Purification and Defilement

Jesus' last encounter with the Pharisees occurs with the curing of the man with the withered hand on the Sabbath (3:1–6). That pericope ends with the Pharisees colluding with the Herodians to put Jesus to death. Now, with his fame spreading, Jesus tangles with the Pharisees again. The details that Mark provides on Jewish purity laws strongly suggest that there were a sufficient number of Gentiles in the Markan community who would need such an explanation.

Purity codes in various cultures develop as a way for a community to ensure life. By trying to set a border between things that bring death and those that bring life, peoples establish boundaries, almost arbitrarily, to keep life within and death out, even if that life is only to ensure the continuity of the community. In the Jewish life of the day, the purity codes were seen as coming directly from God. Consequently, to transgress purity was to sever oneself from God and therefore threaten personal and communal well-being. Jesus' actions and commentary do not abolish the purity codes inasmuch as they reinterpret them.

First, he displays the serious shortcomings that this particular Pharisaic attitude of observing external purity has caused and explains that such a problem has existed throughout the tradition (Mark 7:6–13). Second, his explanation to the disciples gives a new definition to purity. By thought, word, and deed do persons make themselves pure or impure. Mark includes an editorial comment on the ramifications of Jesus' new teaching: Jesus has "declared all foods clean" (7:19). Thus, the goodness of creation is reaffirmed and reclaimed for life, goodness, and God; Satan and his realm of death have no permanent hold whatever.

## Mark 7:24–30, Tyre and the Syrophoenician Woman

Jesus acts according to his new teaching on purity. Mark explicitly states that Jesus goes "from that place" to Tyre, where he secretly enters a house. Judging from his last discourse with the disciples, he apparently was not afraid that the authorities would find out that he had flagrantly violated purity laws.

The city of Tyre lay along the Mediterranean coast in present-day Lebanon. A Phoenician town made wealthy by sea trade, its reputation has a mixed record within the OT tradition. In the books 1 Samuel through 2 Chronicles, Hiram, the king of Tyre, is chiefly lauded for providing workers and building materials to David and Solomon when they constructed the palace and the temple, respectively. The psalmist largely sings Tyre's praises, although in Ps 83:8 Tyre is seen as an enemy. The prophets roundly condemn Tyre for its arrogance and heap all judgment upon it (e.g., Isa 23; Ezek 26–28). During the Maccabean wars, Tyre joined forces with the other Hellenistic nations and fought against Judah. By the intertestamental period, Tyre had become a symbol of Gentile life and therefore antithetical to everything Jewish. In spite of this record, all three Synoptic writers mention Tyre. Matthew (15:21–28) and Mark (7:24–30) have Jesus visiting there, and Mark (3:8) and Luke (6:17) describe people from that city flocking to see him. From these citations we can surmise that a ministry to the Gentile regions of Tyre (and Sidon), either by Jesus or by first-century Christian missionaries, was not unknown.

A question arises in this passage. If Jesus goes to Tyre of his own accord, and in fact, willingly enters a house there, why would his reaction to the Syrophoenician woman be so strong? On the level of the Markan redaction, the answer seems to be that Mark uses the incident to make a statement about the role and position of Gentiles within the Jewish-Christian community in Rome. The journey to Tyre comes immediately after the dispute about ritual purity. The woman's answer to Jesus (7:28) shows the Jewish-Christians in Rome why they should accept a Gentile into their midst. Simultaneously, Jesus' riposte to her (7:29) demonstrates how those without the Law and the Prophets to guide them can nonetheless have the proper disposition to approach him. Finally, if by his actions Jesus can declare "all foods clean" (7:19), by his interchange with the Syrophoenician woman he says the same thing about all human beings. Because purity laws and customs within all human societies separate the elements of life from those of death, and since in Jewish circles death is the realm of sin and Satan, Jesus reclaims another portion of creation for God in expelling the unclean spirit from the Syrophoenician woman's daughter.

## Mark 7:31–37, The Decapolis

Jesus continues his journey in pagan regions from Sidon to the Decapolis. Situating the healing of the deaf-and-dumb man right after expelling the demon from the Syrophoenician girl exemplifies the interconnection between demonic possession and physical infirmity. The people in the Decapolis are astounded at Jesus' ability to restore the man's hearing and speaking. The verb used is ἐκπλήσσομαι (7:37); unlike ἐξίστημι (6:51), it means overwhelming amazement without the notion of being beside oneself.[36] Because the Gentiles in the Decapolis are not expecting a Messiah, questions of Jesus' identity do not arise in the same manner as they would for the disciples or even for the Jews.

---

36. See Matt 7:28; 19:25; 22:33; Mark 1:22; 6:2; 7:37; 10:26; Luke 4:32; 9:43; Acts 13:12.

## Mark 8:1–26, Feeding Four Thousand and Curing a Blind Man

The feeding of the four thousand, the demand for a sign, warning about the leaven of the Pharisees, and the curing of the blind man at Bethsaida — these form a recapitulation of Jesus' ministry so far. The feeding of the four thousand sets the tone for the remaining three passages. As the second of two miraculous feeding stories, it reemphasizes the life-giving promise Jesus holds out to the world. In the midst of this miracle and the many others surrounding it, the Pharisees still seek a sign from heaven (8:11–13).

Jesus' uses the term "generation" in a manner not associated with age or birth.[37] Rather, "generation" describes an attitude of not recognizing Jesus' lordship over creation; instead, members of "this generation," by trusting and crediting their own practices, are actually descendants of a blinded generation. If they cannot recognize signs in the healing, curing, and expelling done in Jesus' name, they will never be able to see any sign of the promise of his lordship.

The admonition about the leaven of the Pharisees and Herod (8:14–21) draws on both the imagery and actions of the miraculous feeding in Mark 8:1–10. The bad leaven is, of course, the leaven exemplified by the Herodians and Pharisees seeking a sign from heaven but blind to the signs already occurring around them.[38] Since the disciples have a hard time making the connection, Jesus' metaphor falls flat on their ears.

The blind man of Bethsaida and those who guide him (8:22–26) consist of those not of "this generation" (8:12). The paradox is apparent. Being blind, his faith allows him to see Jesus. For this reason, Jesus enjoins him to keep the miracle quiet (8:26). The Pharisees and Herodians, on the other hand, can physically see, but their lack of faith has made them blind to the promise Jesus holds out to the world. They will never discover the "messianic secret."

## Mark 8:27–30, Peter's Confession

Peter's declaration about Jesus opens a major turning point in Mark's Gospel, which includes the transfiguration (9:2–13). The setting of Caesarea Philippi has an important role to play in the confession. Lying at the foot of Mount Hermon, itself filled with many ancient sanctuaries to pagan gods, Caesarea Philippi is situated at a series of caves which at the time issued water, thus becoming the major source of the Jordan River. Since caves were perceived as doors to the nether regions, the ancients often considered them sacred. In the Hellenistic world, Pan was the god of the underworld, and Caesarea Philippi had many shrines to his cult.

---

37. See Mark 8:38; 9:19; 13:30.
38. A similar situation occurs with Herod in Luke 23:8.

Jesus poses the question of his identity to the same disciples who had witnessed his many healings and explusions, where demons declared his divinity; they had asked themselves a similar question at the calming of the storm (4:41), and even had participated in his ministry (6:7–13). Now as they pass through an area filled with sanctuaries to false gods, Jesus wants his closest followers to declare his identity. The question is addressed to the whole group, but only Peter answers, "You are the Messiah" (8:29). Unlike Matt 16:16, in which Peter explicitly declares Jesus' divinity as "the Son of the living God," or even Luke 9:20, in which Peter specifies that Jesus is "the Messiah of God," here Peter simply states, "You are the Messiah."

This point is the first time the reader encounters the title "Messiah" since the opening line of Mark's Gospel (1:1, "Christ"). Its resurfacing in this setting gives import to this declaration about Jesus being God's anointed. The appearance of "Messiah/Christ" here, before the Sanhedrin (14:61), and at the cross (15:32) are three of the most significant passages in the Gospel, for Mark is intentionally redefining the title with reference to Jesus. For Mark, to be the Messiah involves suffering, and suffering that cannot be understood outside the mystery of the cross. The following passion prediction makes this point clear.

### Mark 8:31–9:1, First Passion Prediction

Jesus makes plain the ramifications of his role as Messiah and the consequences for those who follow him. The Messiah must undergo an absolute debasement entailing suffering, rejection, and death from the leaders of the society. The last part about rising after three days, the exact opposite to the debasement, goes unnoticed by the disciples. For them, the Messiah is supposed to even the score by avenging and crushing the opposition, which in this case would be the Romans and their accomplices. If such does not occur, Jesus, in their minds, cannot be the Messiah. Peter, once again speaking for the group, realizes this central point when he remonstrates to Jesus (8:32).

Jesus responds to Peter's protestations by calling him "Satan" (8:33). That he has such a strong reaction indicates that Peter touches a real nerve; the apostle is no different from Satan, whom Jesus encountered in the desert right after his baptism (1:12–13). Jesus' rebuke of Peter becomes a confirmation of his own messianic identity and mission. After expelling unclean spirits and demons from countless people, Jesus now manifests the full reason for his existence; he has come to reclaim the world from Satan, and Peter has just sided with that enemy. The rest of Jesus' discourse further defines this central feature.

Jesus' explanation to the disciples presents a great paradox that interplays between perception and reality: To lose is actually a gain, and to gain is actually a loss. As difficult as it is to follow such a way, the disciples, who have been following him right along, are invited to go the full course (8:34). Jesus explains why this road of his is the better path, despite its apparent absurdity (8:35–38).

The rhetorical question in verse 36 speaks about the whole created order or universe with its use of κόσμος. In the Hellenistic setting, to which the Jewish world was not immune, to gain the cosmos would mean to have not only the goods thereof but also the secret of life. Here Jesus says then that life does not originate in the created order itself, but in something or someone beyond it, and the only way to have access to life and its Creator is by not allying oneself with the unredeemed creation.[39]

Jesus returns to the dichotomy he first mentions in Mark 8:12 with the term γενεά (generation), and that is an attitude antithetical to Jesus' lordship. Those seeking life within and according to the ways of the cosmos surely will not find it (8:38). His conclusions evoke a vision of a reality beyond creation. When he comes again, it will be in the glory of his Father surrounded by the holy angels, in the fullness of the realm of God — the opposite of the expectations of the current "generation" (8:38–9:1).

## Mark 9:14–29, Expulsion of a Mute Spirit

This passage has a relation to passages depicting other healing or expulsion accounts as well as to Peter's declaration and Jesus' transfiguration. This healing of the boy with the unclean spirit has two puzzling scenes, each featuring a reprimand. The first involves the disciples and the second includes the father.

The disciples try unsuccessfully to drive out the spirit (9.18), which causes their argument with the scribes. Their inability to do so exasperates Jesus, who attributes their failure to their lack of faith. When Jesus sees the boy's convulsions, the father gives the history of the problem and asks whether Jesus is "able" to provide assistance in the matter (9:22 NRSV). Jesus then rebukes the father for his lack of faith, and the father responds with a cry for more faith, which in itself is a sign of faith. Jesus rebukes the mute spirit, which comes out. The disciples, who seemingly were doing everything they were instructed to do in their mission (6:7–13), are perplexed by their lack of power over the mute spirit. Jesus' response gives the key to understanding the situation.

Because they were not attentive to prayer, the disciples' actions are based on their own power and position and not on the life in Christ. Throughout the Gospel, the stress lies on following Jesus, not working independently of him. The boy's father, too, does not initially see the connection between his request for his son and a life based on the cross. In driving out the spirit and reclaiming the boy

---

39. His argument, then, runs counter to those philosophies championed by the Mithras cult.

from Satan, Jesus wants to reaffirm that his battle against Satan is dependent on his life, and the power of that life is the cross. In the succeeding verses, Jesus' foretelling of his own passion for the second time makes this point clear (9:30–32). Moreover, this expulsion is the last miracle Jesus performs until he comes to Jericho in 10:46. Everything from here until that point consists of teaching on how to interpret his ministry thus far.

## Mark 9:31–37, Second Passion Prediction and True Greatness in Discipleship

The passion prediction and the teaching on greatness secure the relationship that Peter's confession, Jesus' first prediction, and the transfiguration have with Jesus' ministry. For the second time Jesus warns what will happen to him in Jerusalem. The disciples remain silent, and no one questions him about it. After witnessing Jesus' reaction when Peter remonstrated with him at the first prediction, the disciples here no doubt are most reticent to protest his view of the situation or even to ask for clarification. Instead, their conversation launches in another direction antithetical to everything Jesus has said about discipleship up to this point.

In Hellenistic society, respect came only with power, and slavery was the expression of that power. Slaves came from the ranks of conquered populations, but someone or even whole families could be sold into slavery to pay off their debts. The powerless slaves served others, and their powerful owners were served. To say then that to gain respect and prestige one must become a slave and serve is a reversal of societal expectation and runs against the current of all right thinking. Yet, the debasement of becoming a slave is exactly what Jesus means by each of his passion predictions and by the lesson in driving out the mute spirit from the boy (9:14–29). One cannot be a disciple without tying one's life intimately with Jesus.

Jesus' actions with the child provide an example of what he means by his preaching. Children are among the most vulnerable members of any society whose security and position are based on whether or not they have parents. Even a child, however, deserves the respect and dignity Jesus offers. Likewise, someone recognizing such respect and dignity within those whom the child represents does so in Jesus' name and is thereby a true disciple. Jesus continues and brings the lesson home by pointing beyond himself. To receive Jesus is to receive the one who sends him (9:37).

Hearing these words, the early community will recall the voice from heaven at the two occasions in Mark's Gospel, the baptism (1:9–11) and the transfiguration (9:2–13). In turn, they would see Jesus' own humiliation in taking up his mission as the Son of God.[40] It might not be pressing the point too much to observe that Jesus uses a child as a referent and example in this discourse.

## Mark 9:38–41, In Jesus' Name

The discussion on deeds in Jesus' name continues in this pericope. Evidently, wandering preachers or miracle workers unaffiliated with Jesus have made their rounds as well. That they are expelling demons in Jesus' name shows how renowned his mission has become. This description could also reflect problems within the early Christian movement, where missionaries from one community were venturing into areas evangelized by another, a situation that Paul addresses.[41] The only parallel to the saying lies in Luke 9:49–50.[42] Nonetheless, Mark is emphasizing that true discipleship must be accomplished in Jesus' name.

## Mark 9:42–50, A Warning

Jesus' disciples will also form and gather disciples, a heavy responsibility. Someone who sins in the name of Jesus receives a strong warning. The admonition against the temptation to sin begins with children as the topic of discussion. The setting is still Galilee. The rather harsh measures invoked to prevent falling into sin are hyperbole, which overstates the point to make the point. Just as salt cannot become insipid and still be salt, so too the disciple cannot cease to foster the connection with Jesus and his name and still be a follower. Furthermore, Jesus the Messiah is the binding force for all disciples (9:41), which keeps peace among all (9:50)

## Mark 10:1–16, Questions on Divorce

The scene has moved from Galilee to Judea, across the Jordan River into territory ruled by the Roman procurator, Pontius Pilate. These two groups, children and Pharisees along with the latter's respective teachings, play off each other. The Pharisees come to Jesus in order to test him (10:2). No matter which way Jesus responds, they can quote the law to support their case against him. Jesus knows the trap and gets out of it by exposing it.

The plotting and the conniving of the Pharisees are immediately juxtaposed with the innocence and candor of the children. To the guileless children belongs the kingdom of God, and those wishing to enter ought to be just as guileless. This juxtaposition draws from Jesus' teaching, and he voices it in his reprimand and

---

40. Mark 1:1; 3:11.

41. See 1 Cor 1:12; 3:4–5, 22; also see Acts 19:1–7.

42. As a Gospel written primarily for Gentiles, Luke would more likely include this saying than Matthew, who was centered on the Jewish audience, and therefore would want to be careful in admitting missionaries from outside the community.

explanation to Peter and the others (8:31–38). The world of Satan succeeds in all the ways that foster self-aggrandizement at the expense of others, which is what the Pharisees are trying to do. For a person caught in such a way of living, to let go of the pretense would involve a real act of humility of the kind seen only in children.

## Mark 10:17–31, Rich Man

The key to understanding the story of the rich young man is seen in the last verse: "Many that are first will be last and (the) last will be first" (10:31). No doubt the man has obeyed all the commandments and kept them well. We may even conclude that he has found his wealth honestly, or else he would not be so enthusiastic to seek out Jesus. His downfall, however, lies in his own presumption. Salvation does not depend on how well he has achieved his status, either social or religious, but rather on how he has depended on his own efforts to reach it. His reaction shows that he places his trust in himself rather than abandoning that self to trust in God (10:22). Jesus' explanation with the parable of the camel underscores the lesson. The onus for not entering the kingdom of God lies with those who cannot unburden themselves of their wealth and status. To follow Jesus means to humble oneself in order to be exalted (10:31).

## Mark 10:32–45, Third Passion Prediction and True Discipleship

As with the preceding two passion predictions (8:31–32; 9:31–32), this third one is well placed. Jesus' encounter with the rich man demonstrates the futility of self-interest for salvation as it prepares for the upcoming dispute among the disciples. This passion prediction shows the same pattern as the other two. Whenever Jesus states that he must suffer, die, and rise after three days, there is incomprehension on the part of one or more disciples. Jesus then calls them all together and further explains his life and mission. Peter challenges Jesus in the first instance (8:32–33), each disciple asserts himself before the others in the second (9:33–34), and the sons of Zebedee request honored status in the third. In each case, Jesus elucidates his previous statement, and although each of these explanations is similar, none is the same.

In the first case prompted by Peter's protestations, Jesus speaks about the cross. A disciple should pick up the cross and follow him, for those who lose their lives for his sake and the gospel's, save them. This path is the only one to true glory (8:34–38). In the second occurrence with the disputing disciples, Jesus presents the paradox that those wishing to be the first of all must be the last and servant of all, and he uses the example of a guileless child to make his point (9:33–37). Finally, in this third instance, Jesus presents a challenge to James and John. They readily agree to drink from his cup and submit to his baptism, but they do not understand what such a request fully entails. The question of glory recurs as the other disciples become aware of the conversation two of their number are having with Jesus. In his response, Jesus compares rulers of the nations with the kind of rulers his disciples should be. Reiterating the lesson flowing from the second prediction, he relates that the greatest must become the servant of all. In a simple sentence and for the first and only time in Mark's Gospel, Jesus then states the whole purpose of his life and ministry: "For the Son of Man did not come to be served but to serve and to give his life as a ransom for many" (10:45).

Taken as a whole, the three passion predictions present the context of Jesus' ministry. They tell the reader that loss is really gain, humiliation is really glory, and the least is really the greatest. Such a paradox can only exist and such a transformation can only come about by picking up the cross and following Jesus, a move that makes sense only because Jesus' ransom makes it possible.

### Mark 10:46–52, Curing Blind Bartimaeus

The Markan portrayal of Jesus' journey to Jerusalem is more modest than the Lukan one. Whereas the latter early on informs the reader of Jesus' intent to fulfill his destiny in that city, the Markan narrative simply drops a few place names in describing the progress of the journey. The first occurs with mention of the "district of Judea" (10:1), and the second appears here with the reference to Jericho, the city where the road from Galilee turns for the climb through the mountains and terminates in Jerusalem. Although both Matt 20:29–34 and Luke 18:35–43 each have parallel accounts situated in Jericho, neither Matthew nor Luke names the blind man, and indeed, Matthew features two blind men. The uniqueness of the Markan account, therefore, is most important for understanding this particular Gospel.

The name "Bartimaeus" is a fusion of the Greek "Timaeus" and the Aramaic prefix "Bar," meaning "son of." Not only is it curious to have such a name within a Jewish setting, but it also becomes even more so by other circumstances associated with it. Mark, writing in Greek, identifies the blind man as the son of Timaeus but then gives him the proper name, Bartimaeus, which is an Aramaic translation of the Greek. Furthermore, "Timaeus" is not only a Greek name; it also is a title of one of Plato's works, a name that appears nowhere else in either the OT or NT. This whole pericope is the subject of chapter 9 (below), which addresses the name "Bartimaeus," discipleship, and Markan Christology.

Bartimaeus follows Jesus to Jerusalem, the city of Jesus' passion, death, and resurrection. As here, Mark often signals discipleship by exhibiting this act of following Jesus with the verb ἀκολουθέω.[43] The disciples are important to the

---

43. Mark 1:18; 2:14–15; 5:24; 6:1; 8:34; 9:38; 10:21, 28, 32, 52; 11:9; 15:41; but see also 14:51, 54.

structure and content of Mark, with every major section beginning with a discipleship pericope.[44] The Bartimaeus passage is often categorized as a "transitional giving-of-sight story," which bridges the journey to Jerusalem with the ministry in Jerusalem.[45] Based on the Markan use of ἀκολουθέω and the role discipleship has within the whole Markan framework, however, we cannot overlook the fact that Mark 10:46–52, while serving as a transitional scene, is also a lesson about discipleship, and Bartimaeus has a major role this Gospel's narrative. Indeed, he is a model disciple for readers to imitate. The question is how readers or hearers in first-century Rome would respond to a disciple named Bartimaeus.

## Précis

Through Jesus' earthly ministry, the cosmic battle with Satan is joined. To portray this battle, Mark addresses divine communication, divine authority, eschatology, the messianic secret, and discipleship.

---

44. Donahue and Harrington, *Mark*, 30.
45. Ibid., 49.

## Chapter 4

# Passion, Death, and Resurrection in Mark

The passion, death, and resurrection are Jesus' triumph over Satan in the cosmic battle. This triumph sweeps in the eschaton. Creation is saved and reunited with God.

## Mark 11–16

With the turn onto the Jerusalem road at Jericho, we come to the end of the journey to Judea, and with it, the Galilean ministry is completed. Mark writes that Bartimaeus follows Jesus "on the way" (ὁδός, 10:52). Mark wishes to emphasize the *way* of Jesus.[1]

The term, ὁδός, besides meaning "road" or "path," takes on the nuance of "way of life," or "conduct."[2] On this level, within Scripture it represents the manner of life according to God's instruction.[3] By extension, the word came to describe the religious movement associated with Christ's life.[4] Mark certainly intends the concrete notion of "road" as well as the concept of "way of life"; the stress placed on discipleship and following Jesus determines such a conclusion. The question is whether the evangelist also intends to signify that Bartimaeus provides the example of conduct for someone who claims to follow the movement associated with Jesus' name. On this basis, let us approach the passion and resurrection narratives with the eyes of the now-cured Bartimaeus.

## Mark 11:1–11, Entry into Jerusalem

Everything that Jesus has been discussing in his passion predictions and the whole aim of his earthly ministry point to and end up in Jerusalem. Each Synoptic writer

---

1. Both Matthew and Luke, on the other hand, simply say that the blind one(s) follow (ἀκολουθέω) Jesus (Matt 20:34; Luke 18:43).
2. Matt 3:3; 7:14; 22:16; Mark 1:2–3; 12:14; Luke 1:76, 79; 3:4; 7:27; 20:21; John 1:23; 14:4–6.
3. See Isa 40:3.
4. Acts 9:2; 18:25–26; 19:9, 23; 22:4; 24:14, 22.

reports that the crowds place their coats atop the donkey and along the road.[5] Jesus' ministry is centered in Jerusalem until his death. The cheer which the people shout is a paraphrase of Ps 118:25–26. Mark is the only account reading, "Blessed is the kingdom of our father David that is to come!" (11:10).[6] The emphasis in Mark is not on the son of David, a phrase that first occurs with Bartimaeus (10:47–48), but on David the father, a construction used only two other times in the whole NT.[7]

## Mark 11:12–25, Cleansing of the Temple

Mark constructs another intercalation in which the cleansing of the temple is set between the two halves relating the cursing of the fig tree.[8] From Mark 11:12–14, we know that bearing leaves is a sign of the approaching summer, so there should also have been at least unripe fruit, but this tree has nothing. One of the most difficult passages in Scripture, the cursing of the fig tree works by means of subtle analogy. The two violent acts in this section, the cursing of the tree and the cleansing of the temple, are equivalent. The tree is in leaf, and Jesus takes a chance to see if it bears any fruit. It does not, and the curse ensues. When he enters the temple, he expects to see attention focused on the prayer and devotion to which the temple is dedicated, but instead he finds buyers and sellers more interested in their commerce. Jesus' act of driving out the merchants is similar to his cursing the tree, in that they, as representatives of the temple, will never bear fruit. When Peter the next day points out the shriveled tree, he is searching for an explanation. Jesus' answer is somewhat cryptic but not indecipherable.

The fig tree may look dead, but it can still have life within it and produce fruit. Faith that it will do so is necessary. The temple and its cult may appear moribund, but God does not give up on his people, and it too can come back to life. Faith that it will also do so is necessary. As the house of the Deity, temples were considered portals to the divine. For Bartimaeus to see Jesus' dramatic action in the forecourt of the temple would certainly cause him to wonder about the rank of a man who can display such audacity. The next encounter with the scribes, priests, and elders takes up that very question.

---

5. John does not mention this detail (12:12–19). The Synoptic scene echoes 2 Kgs 9:13. There a prophet has anointed Jehu as king and has given him charge of cleansing the house of Israel. John's companions show their support by spreading their garments in front of him and crying out, "Jehu is king."

6. Matthew (21:9) shows, "Hosanna to the Son of David; blessed is he who comes in the name of the Lord"; Luke (19:38), "Blessed is the king who comes in the name of the Lord"; and John (12:13), "Hosanna! Blessed is he who comes in the name of the Lord, [even] the king of Israel."

7. Luke 1:32; Acts 4:25; but see also Matt 1:6.

8. For intercalation, see also Mark 5:21–43.

## Mark 12:1–12, Parable of the Vineyard

The parable of the vineyard and tenants summarizes both Jesus' Galilean and Jerusalem ministries thus far. The various slaves sent to the tenant farmers represent the many prophets who have arisen among the people throughout their history. The landowner of the vineyard is God, and Jesus is his Son. From Bartimaeus's perspective, this parable features another instance in which not only the question of sonship enters the scene, but also one in which there is a description of a father, a father who for all his loving and good qualities, also behaves with such generosity that it is folly.

## Mark 12:13–34, Questioning by Religious and Political Leaders

As a set of disputes involving Pharisees and Herodians first, Sadducees second, and a scribe third, these three discourses are constructed as tests of Jesus' authority. If these members of several established guilds can cause Jesus to stumble in a response, the people will see him with less authority. Only in the last example with the scribe (12:28–34) is there a diminishment of antagonism. In fact, Jesus even compliments the scribe, which indicates that questions in good faith are welcome. However, Jesus sees through and gives little quarter to deviousness and hypocrisy.

## Mark 12:35–37, Son of David

This pericope is the second and final instance in which the phrase "son of David" occurs in Mark's Gospel. Previous to this passage, it arises in Bartimaeus's cry to Jesus along the Jericho road. Unlike the previous three discourses, which are prompted by three different authority figures, Jesus himself rhetorically poses this question to the crowd, which itself becomes a challenge to the scribes. It is based on Ps 110:1 and pursues the simple logic that that reading establishes. In the NT, the title "son of David"[9] reflects the understanding of the day that the Messiah would come from the Davidic line. Jesus' question presses the point. The Messiah still has a connection to David, for according to the tradition, David speaks these lines in the psalm, but Jesus questions the Messiah being the son of David and shows that the Messiah is actually above the earthly monarch.[10] In the Markan

---

9. It occurs most frequently in Matthew's Gospel: 1:1, 20; 9:27; 12:23; 15:22; 20:30–31; 21:9, 15. See also Luke 1:32; 18:38–39; 20:41, 44.

10. The same material appears in Matt 22:41–46 and Luke 20:41–44, using much the same ordering of passages as found in Mark, although Luke lacks the preceding pericope on the Great

Gospel, Bartimaeus is the only individual to use this appellation with regard to Jesus. As one following Jesus into Jerusalem, he hears the crowd calling, "Blessed is the kingdom of our father David that is to come" (11:10).

## Mark 12:38–44, Warning about Scribes

After demonstrating the weakness in the scribal teaching, Jesus denounces their lifestyle, which precludes them from being open to the kingdom of God, thereby highlighting the exceptional quality of the scribe in 12:28–34. Mark uses the account of offerings to the temple treasury as an example of the how the scribes "devour the houses of widows" (12:40).

## Mark 14:1–9, Plot and Anointing

The apocalyptic discourse ends, and the scene immediately shifts to the plot to do away with Jesus. Much of the abstract language found in the apocalyptic narrative will be concretized within the passion; the unfolding events put flesh on this apocalypse. The ominous tone that opens the chapter sets in motion the events to fulfill each of the three passion predictions.[11]

There are no more healing or exorcising miracles after this point, and although the anointing at Bethany does not constitute the customary venue for Jesus' preaching ministry, his encounter with those criticizing the woman functions as the last lesson he speaks to people outside Jerusalem. From this point on, the lesson for his followers is the example of his passion, death, and resurrection, as he picks up the cross and suffers everything it represents.

## Mark 14:10–21, Judas and Passover Preparation

Judas's role in the conspiracy prefaces the Passover account; he too attends the meal, and Jesus lets everyone know that he himself is aware of the plot and knows who is most involved with it. Jesus' directions to the disciples indicate that

Commandment. Yet see Luke 10:25–28. The difference between these two Synoptic accounts and the Markan one is that the latter does not specify to whom the question is directed, unlike Matt 22:41 and Luke 20:41. Furthermore, the term "son of David" occurs in Mark only on the lips of Bartimaeus (10:47–48) and Jesus (12:35); while Matthew uses the phrase throughout his Gospel; Luke, in addition to the cry of the unnamed blind man in 18:38–39 and the verses paralleling these Markan ones, refers to the relationship in Gabriel's annunciation to Mary (1:32). Mark therefore shows a singular use of the phrase "son of David" that is peculiar to this Gospel.

11. Mark 8:31–32; 9:31–32; 10:32–34. The first prediction states that the Son of Man will be handed over to the elders, chief priests, and scribes. The second simply says that he will be turned over into the hands of men. The third mentions the chief priests and scribes who will hand him over to the Gentiles. The plot here shows the chief priests and scribes in conspiracy.

he has already made arrangements ahead of time. His instruction to follow the man with the jar (14:13) is the only time in the whole Markan Gospel where the verb ἀκολουθέω is applied to a situation in which one or more individuals follow someone other than Jesus.[12] The significance of this singular switch of the verb to the person who leads the disciples to the guesthouse augments the importance of the upcoming Passover meal. It is not overstating the point to say that the meal becomes the way in which disciples in the early Christian community follow Jesus.[13] Jesus' harsh words about the betrayer (14:21) reflect the antithetical posture and consequences of one who is invited to follow but who refuses.

## Mark 14:22–31, Passover Meal and Prediction of Peter's Denial

Jesus' action at the Passover meal becomes the symbol of discipleship. The disciples are present at the meal because they have followed Jesus so far. Mark specifies that all drank from the cup. This detail balances the exchange Jesus earlier has with James and John, who ask for chief positions with him in his glory (10:38–39). They all drink, including the sons of Zebedee. Just as this cup leads to the cross for Jesus, so will it too for all of them. The cup of suffering resurfaces in Gethsemane (14:36).

After the three passion predictions within the Gospel, Jesus now gives a veiled foretelling of his torture and death but with a stronger focus on life and resurrection in 14:25. Yes, this is his last meal, but there will be other meals in the future, on the day when he will "drink it new in the kingdom of God." Discipleship entails suffering and death, but it leads to glory. Jesus foretells Peter's denial (14:27–31). In conditions made similar by references and actions to the passion, this passage forms a haunting echo to the reprimand Peter receives after he remonstrates with Jesus after the first passion prediction (8:32–33).

## Mark 14:32–42, Prayer in Gethsemane

The prayer in Gethsemane is full of stress and apprehension. All along Jesus has been exhorting his disciples to follow him, and now the Father asks him to follow his (the Father's) will, all symbolized by "cup" (14:36). Jesus selects Peter, James,

---

12. Ἀκολουθέω occurs twenty times in Mark, and it is used nearly exclusively in terms of discipleship with Jesus.

13. In Mark 16:17, 20 the verb ἀκολουθέω has as its subject the signs that accompany those preaching in Jesus' name. In the secondary conclusion to the Gospel, therefore, "to follow" expresses a relationship of the disciples with Jesus and Jesus with the disciples.

and John to keep watch with him, the same trio chosen to accompany him up the mountain at the transfiguration (9:2–13). There, the disciples are nearly speechless because they are afraid (9:5–6). Here, they sleep and cannot answer because they are so totally unaware of the gravity of the situation (14:40). It is a disappointing scene, but one that has a faint juxtaposition with the transfiguration. At the transfiguration they cannot comprehend the glory they see; in Gethsemane they cannot fathom the extent of the events that are about to transpire. In both cases, Jesus' passion and death form the background.

## Mark 14:43–52, The Betrayal

Judas comes as expected. Through a prearranged signal, a kiss, the betrayer alerts the chief priests, scribes, and elders of Jesus' identity. Each evangelist recounts the story of the cutting of the ear of the chief priest's "servant" (14:47), but the details in each are different. In Mark, Jesus does not correct the would-be defender and does not heal the ear. The result of the Markan portrayal of the situation is a starker narrative, keeping all attention focused on the drama of the arrest. In a contrast to the discipleship of the others, Judas does not follow Jesus figuratively or even literally; rather, he arrives at Gethsemane leading a crowd of thugs. Everyone who up to this point has followed Jesus now abandons him. Without any parallel or allusion in any other Gospel, the notice about the young man who flees away naked is one of the most cryptic passages in the NT. It is the topic of a fuller discussion below.

## Mark 14:53–65, Hearing with the Sanhedrin

Although the young man flees, Peter follows Jesus and the authorities, but "at a distance" (14:54). All three groups — elders, chief priests, and scribes — mentioned in the first passion prediction (8:31–32) are present at this hearing. There is difficulty in finding witnesses whose testimony agrees. Jesus is silent, almost contemptuously so, until asked whether he is "the Messiah, the son of the Blessed One" (14:61–62). His response harks back to the section within Markan apocalypse (13:26–27), which paraphrases the reading from Dan 7:13–14. At this inquiry, however, the reference to Daniel, despite its similar language, is still not an exact quotation. To the chief priest, the allusions and all they entail are threatening enough, and the Sanhedrin use Jesus' own words to condemn him (14:64). The description Jesus gives his disciples in the last prediction of his death (10:34) is fulfilled here. The Sanhedrin "mock him, spit upon him, scourge him, and put him to death."

## Mark 14:66–72, Peter's Denial

In Jesus' first prediction of his passion (8:31–32), Peter immediately challenges him. Jesus then has to correct Peter's perceptions (8:33–38). On the walk to Gethsemane, Jesus foretells the abandonment he will undergo by the disciples (14:27–28). Again, Peter protests by asserting his own fidelity (14:29). Jesus, in turn, predicts Peter's denial (14:30–31), and Peter counters that statement as well.

Mark shows a repetition. In the two instances when Jesus introduces the most demanding parts of being a disciple — suffering, death, and now temptation to betrayal — Peter tries to gainsay him, but Jesus swiftly corrects him.[14] Nonetheless, Mark shows Peter as heeding the corrections, for this apostle does not contradict Jesus after the second and third predictions (9:31–32; 10:32–34). Just as Jesus foretold, Peter denies him. Upon hearing the second cockcrow, Peter recalls Jesus' words with him (14:72). Based on his behavior thus far, it is possible to surmise that Peter weeps for at least three reasons. One, he obviously knows that Jesus was correct in his prediction. Two, he realizes the full import of his denial; and three, he knows that Jesus will indeed be put to death, just as he predicted three times. From this point on, Peter no longer appears in the Markan Gospel, though his name is mentioned by the young man in 16:7.

## Mark 15:1–15, Before Pilate

The elders, scribes, and chief priests are present at the hearing with Pilate, the representative of the Roman state. The gathering of these personages fulfills the prediction Jesus first made about his passion (8:31–32) and the third prediction, that he would be handed over to the Gentiles (10:33). Jesus remains as taciturn before Pilate as he was before the Sanhedrin (14:53–65). Pilate, perhaps expecting Jesus to beg for his life, is amazed at his lack of response. It is difficult to discern whether Jesus is being petulant through his silence or is showing resignation, if not strength, in the face of adversity and death. Pilate would not react in such a manner if he thought that Jesus were being contemptuous in his silence.[15] The evangelist wishes to show disciples how to approach persecution.

Pilate's questioning of the crowd has a cynical side that only adds to the unjust cruelty of his action (15:9–10). Outside the Gospel sources, there is nothing in Roman or Jewish history telling of the release of a prisoner on account of Passover or any other feast. That Barabbas is guilty of murder during a rebellion shows the

---

14. Matthew shows a similar pattern (16:21–28; 26:31–35), but Luke does not (9:22–27; 22:31–34).

15. Nonetheless, in the hearing and trial scenes, Jesus is generally silent in all four Gospels. The Synoptic writers present him as tight-lipped to the point of being belligerent. In John, he answers questions but with a sharp edge in his tone. No doubt there is some historical kernel to this presentation of Jesus' demeanor, which the evangelists write to suit their respective theological purposes.

tense situation existing in Roman Palestine at the time. Releasing him, a known murderer, also augments the degree of Jesus' innocence.

## Mark 15:16–32, Mockery and Crucifixion

The Markan passion displays a gradual but relentless shift from exaltation at the baptism, "You are my beloved Son" (1:9–11), to the humiliation of the death on the cross, at which point a Gentile soldier declares Jesus God's Son (15:39 NRSV). Here, the pagan soldiers demean and ridicule the one who has claimed to be the "Son of Man seated at the right hand of the Power and coming with the clouds of heaven" (14:62).

The crucifixion continues the shift, both in language and in action. As an act of capital punishment, crucifixion was the most ignominious form that the Roman state could mete out, reserved for noncitizens and used primarily on conquered peoples and insurrectionists. Jesus is just about the only proper name associated with crucifixion in the whole historical record of antiquity. Not even the two crucified with Jesus are named.[16] Those condemned were usually stripped naked and then forced to walk to the gibbet carrying at least the crossbeam for their crucifixion. This ordeal was a final act of humiliation, which also weakened the victim physically and psychologically.

All four Gospel accounts include some version describing the dividing of Jesus' clothing. In Mark, however, the casting of lots for Jesus' clothing takes on added significance because verse 24 is another instance of the Greek word ἱμάτιον, a word used in the Bartimaeus pericope, which means "cloak."[17] When Bartimaeus casts off his cloak in 10:50, therefore, he is acting as the disciple who will follow Jesus through every indignity. A sign on the cross for this naked, bloodied man ironically reads, "The king of the Jews" (15:26). Jesus is the subject of absolute mockery, even from those crucified with him. The use of the verb καταβάινω (15:30, 32), "to come or go down," increases the irony in this scene. Jesus is where he is precisely because he has "come down" from an exalted position, and from this position, he is saving himself and others. Indeed, if he were to come down from the cross, true salvation would be null.

## Mark 15:33–41, The Death

The Roman centurion speaks in a manner far different from the passersby, the chief priests, and the scribes (15:25–32), and acts differently from the other Roman

---

16. See Matt 27:38 and Luke 23:32.

17. The term ἱμάτιον also surfaces in Mark 11:7–8; 13:16. The plural form, ἱμάτια, can mean "clothing."

soldiers ridiculing Jesus in 15:16–20. The irony is that Jesus is proclaimed as "God's Son" by the one who presides at his death (15:39 NRSV). Moreover, the presence of the Roman officer at such a critical juncture in the death narrative leads one to wonder whether Mark is staking a claim against the Mithraic mysteries by this centurion's statement. Mark specifies the witnesses to this event. In addition to those named women "looking on from a distance," Mark mentions that many other Galilean women have followed Jesus to Jerusalem (15:40–41). We know that the Twelve all flee at the moment of the arrest in the garden of Gethsemane (14:50), and Mark does not include any men among this group of witnesses at Golgotha.

The evangelist's only use of the term "darkness" occurs at 15:33. Just when the sun is at its brightest, darkness envelopes the whole earth from noon to three o'clock. As others have observed, this period of darkness represents creation's lament over the death of God's Son.[18] The climax of the lament occurs in verse 34: Jesus the Son of God cries in despair, *"Eloi, Eloi, lema sabachthani?"* Jesus, who is on the side of creation and life, has been battling Satan throughout his earthly ministry, wresting creation from Satan's chains.[19] In addition, as a human being, Jesus is a part of creation. Now that the Son of David, the Son of Man, and the Son of God is nailed to the cross, all hope for creation is gone, and Satan with the full extent of his diabolical rule — death, fear, darkness, hopelessness, despair, nihilism — has seemingly vanquished life and hope. Consequently, creation is plunged into the primordial chaos from which God had fashioned the ordered cosmos. As part of that creation, Jesus "cries out with a great cry"[20] on its whole behalf: "My God, my God, why have you forsaken me?" (15:34).

The cry of dereliction causes confusion with the bystanders. The aural similarity between Ελωι and 'Ηλίας leads some to think that Jesus is calling the prophet who is to usher in the Messiah. This question is addressed earlier in Mark (9:11–13), immediately after the transfiguration, and it has direct bearing on the death here. At the transfiguration, Elijah and Moses appear with Jesus. After the voice from the hovering cloud declares Jesus' divine sonship with the Father (9:7), the vision of Moses and Elijah passes, and Jesus is alone with Peter, James, and John. The explanation then begins. The experience on the mountain will not make sense until the Son of Man arises from the dead (9:9). The three disciples explicitly ask Jesus about the scribal tradition holding that Elijah must come first, before the Messiah. Jesus acknowledges the truth of that tradition by replying that Elijah has already come (Mark 9:13).[21] He prefaces his response,

---

18. Donahue and Harrington, *Mark*, 447.
19. Mark 1:13; 4:15; 8:33; and esp. 3:22–30.
20. Author's translation.
21. Matthew (17:13) supplies, "Then the disciples understood that he was speaking to them of John the Baptist." Luke does not have a parallel to Mark 9:9–13, but he covers the issue in 1:17.

however, with a statement tied to the tradition of the Son of Man, who "must suffer greatly and be treated with contempt" (9:12), a direct allusion to his own passion and death, drawing from the prophetic traditions of Ezekiel and Daniel. As such, Mark places more emphasis on the cosmic significance of Jesus' passion, death, and resurrection than he does on the Elijah tradition.

Nonetheless, in this verse we cannot ignore an eschatological element associated with the name of Elijah. He was seen to usher in the messianic age: "Lo, I will send you / Elijah, the prophet, / Before the day of the LORD comes, / the great and terrible day" (Mal 4:5 [3:23]). Jesus is identified with both John the Baptist and Elijah (Mark 6:15; 8:28; 9:4–13), and Christ follows John the Baptist, who was an Elijah figure and entered into martyrdom on account of his fidelity to God.[22]

## Mark 15:42–47, The Burial

The account of Jesus' burial notifies the listener/reader that Jesus was actually laid in a sealed and secured tomb. The qualifying phrase "that had been hewn out of the rock" (15:46) signals that this is a new tomb, which had never seen a previous burial.[23] The detail about the presence of Mary Magdalene and Mary the mother of Joses forms a bridge to the resurrection; these women know exactly where to go to find the body. Joseph of Arimathea wraps Jesus in a linen cloth (σινδών). The only other place this word occurs in Mark's Gospel is with the escaping youth at the arrest (14:51–52).

## Mark 16:1–8, Original Ending of Mark

The same women who witness the death are at the tomb to anoint Jesus. Unlike the resurrection narratives in Matthew and John, Mark does not mention any angels present; Luke (24:4) shows "two men." There is nearly universal agreement among scholars that the original Markan ending concluded with 16:8. The abrupt manner in which the Gospel of Mark ends opened the door for later scribal emendations and corrections. The textual tradition, however, does not support either the longer or shorter endings as original to Mark. Yet, as part of the canonical text of Mark, both the longer and shorter endings serve useful theological purposes.

---

22. Donahue and Harrington make this point as well (*Mark*, 447–48). See also Justin Taylor, "The Coming of Elijah, Mt 17:10–13 and Mk 9:11–13: The Development of the Texts," *RB* 98 (1991): 107–19. See Luke 1:17.

23. The type of tomb constructed at this period is in the *kokim* style. There is a small antechamber from which narrow, carved horizontal shafts radiate. The corpse was then inserted feet or head first.

## *[Mark 16:9–20], Longer Ending of Mark*

The longer ending of Mark, consisting of 16:9–20, surfaces in the Byzantine and the (Western) Bezae texts. Codices Sinaiticus and Vaticanus do not contain it, thereby making certain for most scholars that the longer Markan ending is not part of the original Markan text.[24]

Wherever a passage from one particular Gospel is inconsistent with its parallels in the other Gospels, both early and late scribes try to harmonize the variant texts. An outstanding example is the renditions of the last words of Jesus in Matthew 27:46–50 and Mark 15:34–37. There is also a tendency to elaborate the short accounts of particular events if a scribe feels that information is lacking, as in the Latin and Syriac additions to Luke 23:48.

We can see the scribal emendations comprising the longer ending in four areas. First, the description of Jesus' appearance to Mary Magdalene (16:9–11) is similar to, if briefer than, those accounts in Matt 28:9–10 and John 20:11–18. Second, the longer Markan ending exhibits two verses (16:12–13) that encapsulate the skeleton of the Emmaus pericope in Luke 24:13–35, and by extension also have a faint echo with John 19:25.[25] Third, the commissioning of the disciples (Mark 16:14–18) has parallels with Matt 28:16–20; Luke 24:36–49; John 20:19–23; and even Acts 1:6–8. Fourth, the ascension in Mark 16:19–20 reflects the two ascension passages in Luke 24:50–53 and Acts 1:9–11. The big difference between the two accounts in the Lukan corpus and this Markan one is that the latter explicitly mentions that they go forth to preach and are supported by the Lord's signs (Mark 16:20).

Despite the fact that the longer ending is not part of the original Markan Gospel, it has bearing on the evangelical tradition. The longer ending features Jesus upbraiding the disciples for not believing those who have proclaimed Jesus' resurrection. This information strongly suggests that at the early period in which this section was written, the understanding was that the three women eventually told others about what they had seen and experienced, or at least should have told others about the message the young man at the tomb had given them. Specifically, for the early Markan community, there was no doubt about the resurrection. That the women do not say anything to the disciples as instructed would be for a reason other than fear. This point is developed below.

---

24. This opinion, however, is by no means universal. See M.-É. Boismard, *L'Évangile de Marc: Sa préhistoire* (ÉBib 26; Paris: J. Gabalda, 1994), 237–42.

25. One of the two on the road to Emmaus is named "Cleopas" (Luke 24:18). At the crucifixion in John (19:25) stands "Mary the wife of Clopas." The similarity in the names of Cleopas and Clopas leave many wondering whether the two in the Emmaus pericope are actually Mary and her husband Cl(e)opas.

## Shorter Ending of Mark

The shorter Markan ending (between 16:8 and 16:9 in NRSV) is supported only by italic manuscripts and therefore is much later than the period under discussion.

## Summary

In the Gospel of Mark, the five themes of divine communication, divine authority, eschatology, messianic secret, and discipleship sustain the central feature of Jesus' cosmic battle with Satan.

### Cosmic Battle

The cosmic war between God and Satan begins the moment the Spirit drives Jesus into the desert to be tempted by Satan (1:12–13). Once Jesus begins his ministry, the battle takes place on three fronts with his preaching, healing, and expelling demons. The first passion prediction indicates how the battle ultimately will be won (8:31–32). The great irony of this war occurs in 8:36. Jesus gains the whole world precisely because he forfeits his life to the Father's will.

### Divine Communication

At the baptism (1:9–11) the verb σχίζω describes the rending of the heavens, from which a voice speaks to Jesus: "You are my beloved Son." At the transfiguration the voice from heaven announces Jesus' sonship to Peter, James, and John: "This is my beloved Son. Listen to him" (9:7). Jesus, representing all creation, answers the heavenly voice at the crucifixion: "My God, my God, why have you forsaken me?" (15:34). There is a reprise of the verb σχίζω as the temple curtain tears (15:38). The divine presence is no longer contained within the temple; the cosmos is united with God.

### Divine Authority

Mark establishes the authority of Jesus with the first word in the Gospel, ἀρχή (1:1). Jesus begins his preaching at Capernaum, and while there, he drives out an unclean spirit from a person with an unclean spirit. In both cases, the people remark that, unlike others they have seen and heard, Jesus possesses real authority, or ἐξουσία (1:22, 27). The authority theme continues in 3:13–19; 10:35–45; and 11:27–33.

### Eschatology

Mark explains the difference between the ministry of John and that of Jesus. The former is one of repentance for the forgiveness of sins, and the latter is for repentance and belief in the gospel (1:14–15). The gospel initiates the fullness of time and the approaching kingdom of God. Mark places Jesus' ministry within an eschatological context. The Markan Apocalypse, in chapter 13, comes before the passion narrative and thus establishes the eschatological focus of Jesus' approaching death and resurrection. The realization of the eschaton comes with the women disciples' reaction and response to the news of Jesus' resurrection (16:1–8).

## Messianic Secret

Jesus explains to the disciples that the "secret" is the μυστήριον of the kingdom of God (4:11). Inasmuch as they are privileged to know it, they must walk the path of Jesus all the way to the cross to participate in it. The three titles associated with Jesus — "Son of Man," "Son of David," and "Son of God" — are part of this mystery. Peter clarifies what the titles mean at his confession (8:29), as does the centurion at the cross (15:39).

## Discipleship

To be a disciple entails entering the "mystery of the kingdom of God" (4:11), which involves the same process of humiliation and exaltation that Jesus must undergo, as the three passion predictions make clear (8:31–32; 9:31–32; 10:32–34). Mark links discipleship to baptism with the pericopes about Bartimaeus (10:46–52), the naked young man (14:51–52), and the young man at the tomb (16:5). Discipleship is constitutive of the cosmic battle.

The five themes all surface throughout the cosmic battle that Jesus wins at the resurrection. The eschaton has arrived. The disciples who follow him participate in the same battle but with the assurance that victory has already been won. Ultimately, then, the kerygma in the Gospel of Mark proclaims divine communication and communion.

With these five supporting themes, three Markan pericopes become especially key not only in employing the Greco-Roman worldview of the universe, but also more importantly in demonstrating the salvation of that universe: the baptism of Jesus (1:9–11), the healing of Bartimaeus (10:46–52), and the death and resurrection of Jesus (15:33–16:8). These passages are the subject of the next chapter.

*Part Three*

# Interplay of
# Mithras, Paul, and Mark

## Overview

The Gospel of Mark presents five subsidiary themes of divine communication, divine authority, eschatology, messianic secret, and discipleship within the central thematic focus of Jesus' cosmic battle with Satan. With the resurrection, the eschaton arrives, and Satan — the lord of sin, suffering, and death — is defeated. Jesus' disciples enter into his resurrected life through their baptism, and they too gain victory over Satan. Because his life is resurrected, it also is cosmic. Divine communication becomes divine communion. Three pericopes are essential to developing the Markan cosmology: the baptism, the Bartimaeus pericope, and the death and resurrection account.

God breaks through the heavens and communicates with creation at the baptism, and crucified creation responds to God in despair. The action is symbolized by the tearing of the temple curtain. Between the baptism and the death stands the Bartimaeus pericope. The Bartimaeus account calls into question the whole worldview outlined in Plato's *Timaeus*. The blind son of Timaeus follows the Son of David and discovers at the cry from the cross that the Son of David is the Son of God.

At the resurrection, the Son of God, who has become creation and thus represents creation, is no longer confined by creation. Rather than becoming one with the cosmos, he becomes Lord of the cosmos. Bartimaeus, who follows and sees all this, becomes the model disciple, and like all disciples now living in the eschaton, he becomes one with the Lord.

Plato's *Timaeus* is the foundational worldview for the Greco-Roman civilization. This worldview permeated Jewish circles to greater and lesser degrees. Lease demonstrates that the *magi* of the Zaruthustrian reform were missionaries of the Mithraic cult, and that Cilician pirates were the first to practice this cult in the Roman world.[1] The geographical proximity of the pirates to the Stoical school of Tarsus, and that school's dependence on Hipparchus's discovery of the precession of the equinoxes transformed the cult into a Hellenistic mystery religion. In addition, Tarsus was home to the cult of the Greek god Perseus that became identified with Mithras. Paul, by virtue of his birth and association with Tarsus, inherited the vocabulary and absorbed the philosophy of that city and used it in developing his Christology of the cosmic Christ. A major part of this Christology is the human participation in Christ's life, death, and resurrection.

Paul's association with Rome, through both his preaching and his martyrdom there, influenced the Christian community there. The Gospel of Mark, written

---

1. Gary Lease, "Mithraism and Christianity: Borrowings and Transformations," *ANRW*, Part 2, *Principat*, 23.2 (1980): 1310.

shortly after Paul's death, presents in narrative form a gospel featuring a Pauline Christology.

Any correspondence between the Markan Gospel and Mithraism is most evident in Mark's presentation of Jesus' baptism, death, and resurrection as well as the Bartimaeus pericope. This chapter investigates Mark's presentation of Jesus' baptism. Though only three verses in length (1:9–11), the baptism sets the stage for an evangelical account addressing discipleship, the meaning of the cross, and the cosmological significance of Christ. That its focus on these three areas constitutes a gospel reflecting Pauline theology should not surprise the reader. We know from both Paul's life and his letters that he had a strong influence on the Christian community in Rome.

# Chapter 5

# Mark's Baptism of Jesus

## *Baptism*

[9]It happened in those days that Jesus came from Nazareth of Galilee and was baptized in the Jordan by John. [10]On coming up [ἀναβαίνω] out of the water he saw the heavens being torn open [σχίζω] and the Spirit, like a dove, descending upon him. [11]And a voice came from the heavens, "You are my beloved Son; with you I am well pleased." (Mark 1:9–11)

The Greek verb ἀναβαίνω (1:10), used as a participle, implies that there is a preceding descent into the water on the part of Jesus. Mark tells us that people, acknowledging their sins, came from the Judean countryside and Jerusalem to be baptized in the Jordan River by John (1:5). Further on in Jesus' discourse with James and John, we see that discipleship is inextricably linked with baptism (10:38–39). The story of Bartimaeus's healing, which follows Jesus' discourse with the sons of Zebedee, strengthens the connection between discipleship and baptism.

The development of baptism is difficult to trace. Ritual washing is mentioned with great frequency in the cultic legislation of the OT.[1] Infractions against purity could occur by chance or neglect. In addition, moments within daily living had prescribed ablutions associated with them, for example, at mealtimes. For the religiously observant, therefore, ritual washing was a part of life repeated with great frequency, and infractions were difficult to avoid. No doubt then that the preaching of John the Baptist would resonate with the large elements of the Jewish population.

Although the Jordan River figures prominently in the OT, especially as the Israelites make their way into the promised land, it functions as the waters of purification only with the story of Naaman the Syrian where Naaman is cured of his leprosy (2 Kgs 5:1–14). In the description of that cure, the text reads that

---

1. In the LXX the terms most often used are νίπτω, πλύνω, λούω, καθαρίζω and their related nouns and adjectives, while the Hebrew OT employs רחץ, טהר, and כבס. Although these terms are used mostly within ritual legislation, they are also found in descriptions where cultic and noncultic distinctions are not always clear, e.g., Gen 35:2, טהר, *tāhēr*, "purify."

Naaman "went down" (καταβαίνω) to the Jordan and "plunged" (βαπτίζω) in it seven times (5:14 LXX).

Elsewhere in the LXX, βαπτίζω occurs in three other verses with notions of ritual purity limited to Sir 34:25 and Isa 21:4.[2] This scant textual evidence, limited though it may be, helps to define the purpose of John's baptism and therefore how Jesus' baptism differs from it.

There are elements associated with purity in both John's baptism (1:4–5, 8) and the baptism Jesus offers (10:38–39). As Jesus suggests in Mark 10:38–39, however, his baptism involves something more, which in the context of his earlier passion predictions also has an ominous note. To be baptized in Jesus' baptism entails following Jesus and reducing oneself to a slave (10:44). It may even mean laying down one's life for others (10:45). Jesus' baptism cannot be divorced from discipleship.

## Baptism and Discipleship

The opening quotation in Mark's Gospel is followed by a short description on John's ministry (Mark 1:4). As the account continues, we learn more about the Baptist, a prophetic figure who garners huge crowds with his baptism of repentance.[3] Mark attributes the paraphrased quotation in verses 2–3 to Isaiah. This association with Isaiah elevates John's prophetic stance and secures his position within the divine plan. John turns the focus to another, however, and in comparison sees himself as unworthy. Furthermore, as John proclaims, this person, whom Isaiah calls "the Lord" (1:3), will baptize with the Holy Spirit (1:8).

There are three occurrences associated with Jesus' baptism: the rending of the heavens, the descent of the Spirit, and the voice from heaven (1:10–11). The voice from heaven, speaking in the second person, is only for Jesus to hear and confirms Jesus' divine sonship, first introduced in 1:1. In the Wisdom tradition, this sonship had been long associated with the righteous person.[4] Thus Mark, in addition to linking his account of Jesus to the Isaiah prophecies, also sets it well within Israel's wisdom tradition along with the hope for God's blessing of immortality upon the righteous.[5] God, coming with the Spirit (1:10) has proclaimed

2. The other remaining LXX reference is Jdt 12:7.
3. See also Hugh M. Humphrey, *He Is Risen! A New Reading of Mark's Gospel* (New York: Paulist Press, 1992).
4. The passion narratives in the Synoptic tradition to a great degree follow the narrative line and theological themes found in the Book of Wisdom. Divine sonship is most evident in Wisdom 2, especially 2:13. Against this background, one can see allusions and references to the divine sonship. See Wis 7:7; 8:21; 9:6, 10. See also Michael Patella, *The Death of Jesus* (CahRB 43; Paris: J. Gabalda, 1999), 166.
5. Wis 1:1; 3:1–4; 4:7–14, 16; 5:2, 15; 10:6; 18:7, 20–23.

Jesus as his Son (1:11), and now the Spirit drives Jesus into the desert to be tempted by Satan.

The narrative flow from Jesus' baptism to his temptation in the desert not only associates the two scenes; it also sets the tone and theme for his earthly ministry. The Beelzebul controversy with the Pharisees (3:23–26) is precipitated by Jesus' expelling demons (3:22–30). When this expulsion occurs in the ministry, it is often associated with physical healing;[6] yet driving out demons and unclean spirits also stand on its own.[7] When Jesus chooses the apostles, it is the power to expel that he first gives them, and that power is restated when Jesus sends them out on mission.[8] Hence, Jesus' earthly ministry has a cosmic thrust. The world is in the clutches of a diabolical power in which sickness, suffering, and death are the manifestations of such evil. At the baptism, therefore, the Markan narrative emphasizes the eschatological character of creation's redemption, a redemption that begins at the pouring of water in the name of the Holy Spirit.

## History of Baptism

We know that Jesus is baptized by John, and yet within the Markan narrative Jesus will speak about the baptism with which he is baptized (10:38–39). Is there a difference between John's baptism and the baptism about which Jesus is speaking in this passage? How does the eschatological emphasis of Jesus' ministry relate to both the baptism he has received as well as the baptism with which he will baptize others?

In a detailed study on the origins of Christianity, Justin Taylor and Etienne Nodet research this very topic.[9] The baptism of John gives rise to two questions: Was it a single, unrepeatable act? Or were there multiple and periodic immersions?[10] From elsewhere in the NT, we know that John seemingly has an ongoing ministry of baptism in at least two venues: at Bethany (Bethabara?) "across the Jordan" from Jericho (John 1:28); and farther upstream, at Aenon near Salim Perea (3:23).[11] In addition, two references in the Acts (18:25; 19:3) report the existence of John's baptism well after the Baptist's martyrdom. We can conclude,

---

6. Mark 1:32, 34, 39; 6:13; 7:24–30; 9:17–27, 38.
7. Mark 1:23–27; 5:1–19.
8. Mark 3:14–15; 6:7.
9. Etienne Nodet and Justin Taylor, *The Origins of Christianity: An Exploration* (Collegeville, MN: Liturgical Press, 1998), 57–88.
10. Ibid., 60.
11. Aenon and Salim were located in the Decapolis. If Bethabara is Bethany "across the Jordan," it would have been located in Perea. Both Galilee and Perea were under the Jewish King Herod Antipas. The Decapolis was a group of "free cities."

therefore, that John's baptism was repeatable and not a bestowed charism linked peculiarly to John.[12]

Another set of questions surrounding John arise. Gathering all the NT references of John and his baptism, two interpretations are possible: either John is an apostle of an enclosed group and not its founder, or he is at the center of a popular movement for which baptism is an identifying action.[13] Because of the confusion in the minds of many between John and Elijah (Mark 6:14–16; 8:28), and thus the sense of a realized eschatology, the second interpretation seems untenable, and therefore the first is preferred.[14] This conclusion leads to another question: If John is the "apostle" for an enclosed group, what kind of group was this and how was it distinct from Jesus' following?

John really does not preach any particular doctrine except a return to obeying the Law in light of imminent judgment;[15] in this sense, he stands well within the tradition of many OT prophets. John's distinguishing characteristic is that he administers a baptism. So important is this baptism that after John's death his disciples continue the mission of baptism and preaching to others (Acts 18:24–25; 19:2–4). As a body, John's disciples have a distinct self-identity that survives his death (Mark 2:18–20; 6:29).[16]

From the Fourth Gospel we know that both Jesus and the Baptist performed similar baptismal rituals, which caused confusion among their respective disciples (John 3:23–30).[17] Nonetheless, there were differences between the two, which the readings from Acts also demonstrate (18:24–25; 19:2–4).

Nodet and Taylor, focusing on a line from Ignatius of Antioch, determine how Jesus' baptism would have been differentiated from the baptism of John.[18] In his *Letter to the Ephesians*, Ignatius says that Jesus "was baptized in order that by his suffering he might cleanse the water" (Ign. *Eph*. 18).[19] By this time in the early Christian community, the water had become a symbol of Jesus' redemptive death and part of Christian initiation.[20] Following the baptism the theophany establishes Jesus as the Son of God according to the Spirit as well as makes Jesus the source of the paschal faith in the resurrection (Mark 1:10–11).[21] Looking to John 1:32,

---

12. Ibid., 60–61.

13. Ibid., 70–71.

14. Ibid.

15. Ibid., 72.

16. Ibid., 73. E. Nodet and J. Taylor go on to use Gamaliel's advice in Acts 5:34–39 as a basis on which to judge the enduring quality of the Baptist's disciples.

17. Ibid.

18. Ibid., 74.

19. Michael W. Holmes, ed., *The Apostolic Fathers: Greek Texts and English Translations* (Grand Rapids: Baker Books, 1999), 149.

20. E. Nodet and J. Taylor, *Origins*, 74.

21. Ibid.

where there is only the Spirit and no mention of a rite of baptism, Nodet and Taylor conclude that the Spirit and not the rite distinguishes Jesus' baptism from John the Baptist's.[22]

If by his baptism Jesus becomes John's disciple, the following theophany indicates a major transformation of its conditions. Because the theophany expresses resurrection, the preceding baptism expresses Jesus' death.[23] The theophany, besides being an act of divine communication, also lends a cosmological significance not only to Jesus' baptism, but also to the whole of Mark's Gospel.

The baptism in Mark (1:9–11) is one of two poles in the Second Gospel upon which Markan cosmology stands; the death of Jesus is the other (15:33–41). Linking these two accounts together is the Greek verb σχίζω, which appears only at Mark 1:10 and 15:38. The salient point concerning this verb is that in these two instances it is used to describe the tearing open of two supernatural realities, one in heaven and the other in the temple, thus allowing for access from the heavenly realm to the earthly one. Hence, Mark's Gospel begins on a note of divine communication.[24]

The people come to John the Baptist as they "acknowledged [ἐξομολογέω] their sins" (Mark 1:5), an act that identifies the sin with the sinner.[25] Jesus' baptism extends this reality of sin to its furthest extent in that the sinner is assimilated into death.[26] The water of baptism, an essential part of purification, becomes on another level first a symbol of death, and then once it has effected the purification of sin, it becomes a symbol of the resurrection and the Spirit.[27] Indeed, Paul says as much.[28] There is still yet another symbolic level in Jesus' baptism. Jesus enters into the Law in being baptized by John, since it is the restoration of the Law that John proclaims (1:5). On the surface, the Jordan recalls the entry into the promised land. With Jesus, this entry is transformed into a victory over death.[29]

Other books in the NT make this same point, especially the Pauline writings:[30]

Or are you unaware that we who were baptized into Christ Jesus were baptized into his death? We were indeed buried with him through baptism into death, so that, just as Christ was raised from the dead by the glory of the Father, we too might live in newness of life. (Rom 6:3–4)

---

22. Ibid., 75.
23. Ibid.
24. This topic receives full development below.
25. E. Nodet and J. Taylor, *Origins*, 75.
26. Ibid.
27. Ibid.
28. Ibid., 76.
29. Ibid.
30. Ibid.

That is what some of you used to be; but now you have had yourselves washed, you were sanctified, you were justified in the name of the Lord Jesus Christ and in the Spirit of our God. (1 Cor 6:11)

You were buried with him in baptism, in which you were also raised with him through faith in the power of God, who raised him from the dead. (Col 2:12)

From these selections we can observe that Paul, insisting on human participation in the death of Christ, sees the entry into that participation as coming through baptism. Emphasis on such participation lies at the core of the evolution of the kerygma.[31]

Nodet and Taylor observe that there is no evidence of daily ablutions associated with Christian baptism, and they see two reasons for Christian baptism's singularity. First, Christian baptism is a part of a baptism in the Spirit, which establishes a connection with the death and resurrection of Christ. Second, it is a unique and definitive act that effects the crossover from living in the world outside Christ to living in the world with him. Life therefore conquers death, and all purity codes vanish.[32]

The kerygma predates the written, NT texts. The Pauline writings often show acknowledgement of a preaching ministry existing before any written documents.[33] It is debatable whether the disciples engaged in such work during Jesus' lifetime, or whether the references in the Gospels to their ministry reflect early Christian practices postdating Jesus' death. Nonetheless, the parallel citations in the Gospels describing a preaching ministry suggest that this work existed while Jesus was still alive on earth.[34]

---

31. E. Nodet and J. Taylor (ibid., 83) refer to 1 Cor 1:13–18 as an example. The concept of human participation in the life of Christ will be discussed more fully below.

32. E. Nodet and J. Taylor (ibid., 84–85) refer to Mary Douglas, *Purity and Danger: An Analysis of the Concepts of Pollution and Taboos* (London: Routledge & Kegan Paul, 1966); Jean Soler, "Semiotique de la nourriture dans la Bible," *Annales: Économies, sociétés, civilisations* 28, no. 4 (1973): 943–55; Bruce J. Malina, *The New Testament World: Insights from Cultural Anthropology* (Atlanta: John Knox, 1981).

33. Rom 15:20; 1 Cor 1:23; 2:1; 11:26; 2 Cor 1:19; Gal 1:16; Phil 1:14, 18; Col 1:28; 1 Thess 2:9.

34. Matt 10:5–15//Mark 6:6–13//Luke 9:1–6; Matt 17:16//Mark 9:18//Luke 9:40; Mark 9:38–41//Luke 9:49–50.

## Chapter 6

# Participation in Christ, a Pauline and Markan View

The Pauline writings offer the earliest and clearest description of what participation in Christ means. That the apostle to the Gentiles wrote his texts before the Gospels were penned makes them a window into the theology of the early Christian world, or at least the foundation of the theology that became a dominant one in the Church.

### Romans 5:12–21

[12]Therefore, just as through one person sin entered the world, and through sin, death, and thus death came to all, inasmuch as all sinned — [13]for up to the time of the law, sin was in the world, though sin is not accounted when there is no law. [14]But death reigned from Adam to Moses, even over those who did not sin after the pattern of the trespass of Adam, who is the type of the one who was to come.

[15]But the gift is not like the transgression. For if by that one person's transgression the many died, how much more did the grace of God and the gracious gift of the one person Jesus Christ overflow for the many. [16]And the gift is not like the result of the one person's sinning. For after one sin there was the judgment that brought condemnation; but the gift, after many transgressions, brought acquittal. [17]For if, by the transgression of one person, death came to reign through that one, how much more will those who receive the abundance of grace and of the gift of justification come to reign in life through the one person Jesus Christ. [18]In conclusion, just as through one transgression condemnation came upon all, so through one righteous act acquittal and life came to all. [19]For just as through the disobedience of one person the many were made sinners, so through the obedience of one the many will be made righteous. [20]The law entered in so that transgression might increase but, where sin increased, grace overflowed all the more, [21]so

that, as sin reigned in death, grace also might reign through justification
for eternal life through Jesus Christ our Lord.

In this passage, Paul uses the Old Adam/New Adam typology, which is understood as representing the whole human race. This typology contrasts the sin and
death of Adam with the grace and justification of Christ (v. 17). Adam's sin is
reversed by Christ's obedience, even though this obedience entails suffering and
death. Christians reap the fruit of Christ's salvific act of obedience through his
resurrection and are thereby saved.

## Romans 8:12–17

[12]Consequently, brothers, we are not debtors to the flesh, to live according
to the flesh. [13]For if you live according to the flesh, you will die, but if by
the spirit you put to death the deeds of the body, you will live.

[14]For those who are led by the Spirit of God are children of God. [15]For
you did not receive a spirit of slavery to fall back into fear, but you received
a spirit of adoption, through which we cry, "*Abba*, Father!" [16]The Spirit
itself bears witness with our spirit that we are children of God, [17]and if
children, then heirs, heirs of God and joint heirs with Christ, if only we
suffer with him so that we may also be glorified with him.

With this contrast between life in the flesh and life in the Spirit, Paul develops
a theology of participation. The Christian enters into Christ's life through baptism
(Rom 6:4), which within the context of this letter signifies an ontological change.
The human life becomes Christ's life; if Christ suffers, dies, and rises to eternal
life, so does his baptized disciple.

## 1 Corinthians 15:12–28 (see also 1 Thess 4:13–18)

[12]But if Christ is preached as raised from the dead, how can some among
you say there is no resurrection of the dead? [13]If there is no resurrection of
the dead, then neither has Christ been raised. [14]And if Christ has not been
raised, then empty [too] is our preaching; empty, too, your faith. [15]Then
we are also false witnesses to God, because we testified against God that he
raised Christ, whom he did not raise if in fact the dead are not raised. [16]For
if the dead are not raised, neither has Christ been raised, [17]and if Christ
has not been raised, your faith is vain; you are still in your sins. [18]Then
those who have fallen asleep in Christ have perished. [19]If for this life only
we have hoped in Christ, we are the most pitiable people of all.

20But now Christ has been raised from the dead, the firstfruits of those who have fallen asleep. 21For since death came through a human being, the resurrection of the dead came also through a human being. 22For just as in Adam all die, so too in Christ shall all be brought to life, 23but each one in proper order: Christ the firstfruits; then, at his coming, those who belong to Christ; 24then comes the end, when he hands over the kingdom to his God and Father, when he has destroyed every sovereignty and every authority and power. 25For he must reign until he has put all his enemies under his feet. 26The last enemy to be destroyed is death, 27for "he subjected every-thing under his feet." But when it says that everything has been subjected, it is clear that it excludes the one who subjected everything to him. 28When everything is subjected to him, then the Son himself will [also] be subjected to the one who subjected everything to him, so that God may be all in all.

As in Rom 5:12–21, in this hymn from Corinthians Christ has overcome sin and death, and with his grace, so have Christians (v. 22). Paul elaborates on the topic by discussing the circumstances of those who have already died (vv. 12–19), a topic that is also the theme of 1 Thess 4:13–18. These people, too, are saved by participating in Christ's death and resurrection.

## *Philippians 2:3–11*

3Do nothing out of selfishness or out of vainglory; rather, humbly regard others as more important than yourselves, 4each looking out not for his own interests, but [also] everyone for those of others.

5Have among yourselves the same attitude that is also yours in Christ Jesus, 6Who, though he was in the form of God, / did not regard equality with God something to be grasped. / 7Rather, he emptied himself, / taking the form of a slave, / coming in human likeness; / and found human in appearance, / 8he humbled himself, / becoming obedient to death, / even death on a cross. / 9Because of this, God greatly exalted him / and bestowed on him the name / that is above every name, / 10that at the name of Jesus / every knee should bend, / of those in heaven and on earth and under the earth, / 11and every tongue confess that / Jesus Christ is Lord, / to the glory of God the Father.

The whole action of self-emptying (κενόω, v. 7) in order to be exalted (ὑπερυψόω, v. 9) describes a process of descent and ascent, echoing the movement of Christ's baptism in Mark 1:9–11. Paul is nonetheless establishing an Old Adam/New Adam typology despite the fact that this hymn is often mined for its notions of Christian kenosis.

Perhaps one of the most famous Pauline passages, the Philippians hymn is often the foundational text for the kenotic theology of the preexistent Christ. In that discussion the preexistent Christ is described as engaged in a process of self-emptying in order to take on sin and death. This pouring out is followed by resurrection and lordship over creation. Kenotic theology, then, defines a preexistent Christ who breaks through the heavenly spheres in order to lead people into the heavenly realm.

Although interpreting the Philippians hymn according to kenotic theology is well within the Christian tradition, one is on surer ground in claiming that Paul's writing predates kenotic interpretation and that he is actually referring to the Old Adam/New Adam typology. At this point in Christian history, in other words, kenotic theology is anachronistic. Historians of dogma show that kenotic theology has no origin in the christological debates of the early Christian centuries. Furthermore, a single verse cannot be the sole determinant of a theology, whether or not the theology has roots in antiquity or contemporary times.[1]

## *Colossians 1:11–14*

[11]strengthened with every power, in accord with his glorious might, for all endurance and patience, with joy [12]giving thanks to the Father, who has made you fit to share in the inheritance of the holy ones in light. [13]He delivered us from the power of darkness and transferred us to the kingdom of his beloved Son, [14]in whom we have redemption, the forgiveness of sins.

Colossians 1:11–14 links Christians to the participation in Christ's salvation. In verses 15–20 the hymn continues and connects this participation to the whole cosmos.

The comparison of Pauline passages with the Markan baptismal account strongly suggests that Mark employs certain aspects of Pauline theology within

---

1. See Ralph P. Martin, *A Hymn of Christ: Philippians 2:5–11 in Recent Interpretation and in the Setting of Early Christian Worship* (Downers Grove, IL: InterVarsity, 1997), 67. See also James D. G. Dunn, *Christology in the Making* (Grand Rapids: Eerdmans, 1989), who in his exhaustive study of early Christianity reaches similar conclusions with regard to the Philippians hymn. He claims that in the Philippians hymn Paul uses "Adam language" of the Wisdom tradition and introduces christological phrases and vocabulary that, outside their immediate Wisdom and Adam context, would be understood as ascribing a preexistent role in creation to Christ himself. Dunn cautions, however, that there are insufficient indications that this is what Paul intended. As far as our study is concerned, Dunn sees that the hymns in both Philippians and Colossians reflect a language in transition, "with a meaning that probably grew as the original context and thought culture changed" (255). Nonetheless, Jerome Murphy-O'Connor, "Crucifixion in the Pauline Letters," in *The Cross in the Christian Tradition* (ed. Elizabeth Dreyer; New York: Paulist Press, 2000), states unequivocally that in the Philippians hymn Paul underscores that "Jesus was not sacrificed. He sacrificed himself"; and that Jesus out of love choosing to die by crucifixion is foundational to Pauline theology (28–29), a point developed further below.

the overarching theology of his Gospel. The degree to which Mark actually drew on a Pauline theology held by members of the Christian community in Rome is difficult to determine, for nothing in the textual tradition indicates that there was a sharing of sources. What we are discussing, rather, is a tradition carried by Paul through his writings, presence, and death in Rome.

Paul preached a version of the kerygma upon which Mark based the Gospel. In broad strokes, this kerygma stresses Christ's obedience to death on the cross and his subsequent ascent into glory. The disciple participates in the same descent and ascent through baptism (Mark 10:38–39). The context that encouraged such conclusions leading to Paul's dedication to the kerygma has Jewish roots along with Hellenistic ones. The Christian proclamation, nonetheless, was a unique one in its claims.

## Summary

From each of these hymns, we can conclude that the concept of Christ as the second Adam dominates Pauline christological expressions. This Christology can be seen as "Jesus' complete oneness with fallen man and the dramatic consequence of Jesus' resurrection for mankind — his death understood as the end of the first Adam, his resurrection as the bursting through the cul-de-sac of death to begin a new humanity as last Adam."[2]

Paul employs the Wisdom language of pre-Christian Judaism to demonstrate the cosmic character and significance of the Christ event in its continuity with God's creation and Christ's redemption. Paul understood divine Wisdom as the powerful and beneficent outreach of the transcendent God into his creation with an intention for its redemption. The Christ-event then, for Paul, is God's own action on behalf of the human race.[3]

## Précis

Mark's account of Jesus' baptism involves Jesus descending into the water as well as ascending from it. Immediately, there is an act of divine communication (1:10). As a result, Jesus' baptism also becomes a metaphorical action of death and resurrection. The disciple who wishes to follow Christ and who thus undergoes Jesus' baptism participates in this same death and resurrection. The Gospel of Mark, therefore, gives great prominence to the cross, and in so doing it reflects a strong Pauline theology.

---

2. Dunn, *Christology*, 254–55.
3. Ibid., 255.

## Chapter 7

# Bartimaeus, the Son of Timaeus
# (Mark 10:46–52)

This chapter discusses Markan vocabulary, the name "Bartimaeus," discipleship, and Markan Christology.

> [46]They came to Jericho. And as he was leaving Jericho with his disciples and a sizable crowd, Bartimaeus, a blind man [τυφλός], the son of Timaeus, sat by the roadside begging. [47]On hearing that it was Jesus of Nazareth, he began to cry out and say, "Jesus, son of David [Υἱὲ Δαυίδ], have pity on me." [48]And many rebuked him, telling him to be silent. But he kept calling out all the more, "Son of David, have pity on me." [49]Jesus stopped and said, "Call him." So they called the blind man, saying to him, "Take courage; get up, he is calling you." [50]He threw aside his cloak [ἱμάτιον], sprang up, and came to Jesus. [51]Jesus said to him in reply, "What do you want me to do for you?" The blind man replied to him, "Master, I want to see." [52]Jesus told him, "Go your way; your faith has saved you." Immediately he received his sight [ἀναβλέπω] and followed [ἀκολουθέω] him on the way.

### The Bartimaeus Passage

The name "Bartimaeus" (10:46), a combination of the Aramaic prefix *bar*, meaning "son of," with a Greek proper name, "Timaeus," has been the source of much speculation and debate. In the Gospel text, Mark translates the name into Greek but does not do so for any other Jewish or Aramaic name, such as Mary, Jairus, or even Jesus. Some conclude that no known Semitic name could furnish the root for the name "Timaeus"; yet they hold that a connection with the figure from Plato's writings "seems unlikely."[1] One can make a strong case, however, that a reference to Plato's *Timaeus* is precisely the reason why Mark alone cites this individual as well as translates his name.

---

1. John R. Donahue and Daniel J. Harrington, *The Gospel of Mark* (SP 2; Collegeville, MN: Liturgical Press, 2002), 317.

## Background

This singular occurrence of the term "Bartimaeus" has led to a good deal of study in modern scholarship on the origins of this whole pericope.

Based on the third-person plural verb form of ἔρχομαι in 10:46, and the singular masculine participle form ἐκπορεύομαι in the following sentence, there is the suggestion that in the pre-Markan tradition, 10:46–52 was independent of 10:35–45.[2] This argument holds that it would make more sense if the complete subject (καὶ τῶν μαθητῶν αὐτοῦ καὶ ὄχλου ἱκανοῦ) were set in the first sentence rather than the second, in verse 46.[3] The awkward style of verse 46 indicates that it was added to the pericope in order to make it more consistent within its immediate context.[4] Furthermore, the construction ὄχλος ἱκανός (v. 46) is necessary in order to maintain the smooth flow into 11:1–11.[5] As pre-Markan material, the pericope itself does not mention whether anyone specifically informed Bartimaeus about Jesus' presence; verse 47 merely uses the singular masculine participle ἀκούσας. The indefinite subject πολλοί simply indicates a redactional seam.[6]

As for the phrase ὁ υἱὸς Τιμαίου Βαρτιμαῖος, there are two schools of thought regarding its origin. Dibelius, Bultmann, Nineham, Robbins, and others see the patronymic Bartimaeus as a secondary addition to the passage; Johnson, Schmid, Taylor, and Kertelge think it more plausible to see the proper name as a reminiscence.[7] Is the phrase ὁ υἱὸς Τιμαίου a translation for Greek-speaking readers of the Aramaic name "Bartimaeus"? Mark often translates any Aramaic or other foreign terms with the phrase ὅ ἐστιν and sets the definition after the word instead of before it (3:17; 7:11, 34; 12.42, 15.16, 42). On this basis, we can conclude that the pericope with the name "Bartimaeus" originated among Greek-speaking Christians when it eventually came to Mark.[8] No one in Mark's community may have known a Bartimaeus, but the employment of his name reflects Mark's tendency to rely on the tradition wherever possible.[9]

---

2. Earl S. Johnson Jr., "Mark 10:46–52: Blind Bartimaeus," *CBQ* 40 (1978): 191.

3. Ibid., 192.

4. Ibid., 192–93.

5. Ibid., 193.

6. Ibid.

7. Johnson, "Bartimaeus," 193, citing Rudolf Bultmann, *Die Geschichte der synoptischen Tradition* (Göttingen: Vandenhoeck & Ruprecht, 1957), 228; Martin Dibelius, *From Tradition to Gospel* (London: Nicholson & Watson, 1934), 52–53; Karl Kertelge, *Die Wunder Jesu im Markusevangelium: Eine redaktionsgeschichtliche Untersuchung* (Munich: Kösel, 1970), 179; Dennis E. Nineham, *Saint Mark* (Philadelphia: Westminster Press, 1978), 285; Vernon K. Robbins, "The Healing of Blind Bartimaeus (10:46–52) in the Marcan Theology," *JBL* 92 (1973): 232; Josef Schmid, *The Gospel According to Mark* (Staten Island, NY: Alba, 1968), 202; Vincent Taylor, *The Gospel according to Mark* (2nd ed.; London: Macmillan, 1966), 446, 448.

8. Johnson, "Bartimaeus," 193.

9. Ibid., 193–94, citing Ernest Best, "Mark's Preservation of the Tradition," in *L'évangile selon Marc: Tradition et rédaction* (ed. M. Sabbe; Louvain: Leuven University Press, 1974), 21–34; Rudolf Pesch, *Das Markusevangelium* (Freiburg: Herder, 1976), 1, 15–31.

## Markan Vocabulary

Any discussion on the Zeitgeist of NT writings must include OT literature. The audiences for the NT Epistles and Gospels, if not Jewish-Christians, would have been Gentiles or God-fearers who were at least somewhat familiar with the OT thought and writings.[10] The dispersion of Jews throughout the major cities of the Roman Empire — Antioch, Damascus, Alexandria, Ephesus, Corinth, and Rome — itself would have ensured that the many Gentiles would have at least a passing knowledge of Jewish thought. Moreover, the strength of Hellenistic civilization was its ability to absorb and transmit cultures across the borders of various nation-states. The Bartimaeus story, therefore, also would resonate with listeners familiar with Jewish Scripture and tradition during the Hellenistic period, and four terms in particular further this assessment: "blind" (τυφλός), "Son of David" (υἱὸς Δαυίδ), "see again/receive sight" (ἀναβλέπω), and "follow" (ἀκολουθέω).

## Blindness and Sight

For the Greco-Roman world, curing of blindness was one of the most popular healing miracles.[11] The evidence suggests that in the Jewish world curing blindness would have been held in equally high regard, particularly since restored sight is seen as an attribute of the eschaton.[12] In the LXX τυφλός takes on various meanings. Most often "blind" or "blindness" is used as a metaphor for suffering, evil, sin, or a curse.[13] Blindness is both a simile and a metaphor for confusion.[14] As such, people are supposed to show charity and compassion to the blind.[15] On the other hand, blindness, as a cultic defect, prevents people from taking part in temple worship;[16] yet the Lord takes responsibility not only for allowing sight but

---

10. "God-fearers" refers to Gentiles drawn to Judaism, a term translating two phrases appearing in Acts: φοβούμενος τὸν θεόν (Acts 10:2, 22, 35; 13:16, 26) and σεβόμενος/σεβομένη τὸν θεόν (Acts 13:43, 50; 16:14; 17:4, 17; 18:7). It is difficult to determine the size of such a group in the Hellenistic world, however, without more evidence of their existence outside the book of Acts.

11. Barry Blackburn in *Theios anēr and the Markan Miracle Traditions* (WUNT 40; Mohr [Siebeck] Tübingen, 1991), 96, cites various pre-Christian Hellenistic texts featuring gods curing the blind. Predominant among them is Asclepius, who is recounted in Epidauran inscriptions as well as in works of Menander and Aristophanes. Asclepius's reputation in this capacity continued into the Christian period, while Isis was credited with the same healing powers at Christianity's outset. Even Vespasian and Hadrian have such cures associated with them.

12. Isa 29:18; 35:5; 42:7, 16, 18; 61:1 LXX; Jer 31:8.

13. Exod 23:8; Deut 16:19; 28:29; Sir 20:29; Zeph 1:17; Zec 11:17; Isa 59:10.

14. Deut 28:29; Isa 59:10; Zeph 1:17.

15. Lev 19:14; Deut 27:18.

16. Lev 21:18; 22:22; Deut 15:21; Mal 1:8. As a cultic defect, blindness precludes participation in temple worship. It did not ostracize one from the community, however, unlike leprosy, which was an impurity. See below.

also for causing blindness.[17] Physical sight is juxtaposed with spiritual blindness and vice versa.[18]

Within this prophetic tradition, Isaiah best expresses the relationship between physical blindness and spiritual sight. The servant in Isa 42:19 is praised for being blind and deaf while simultaneously showing dedication to the Lord and spiritual insight. The Septuagintal version of Isa 61:1 in particular has direct resonance with Mark 10:46–52.

A construction included in Isa 61:1 but not present in the MT Hebrew is the phrase τυφλοῖς ἀνάβλεψιν, a version of the very phrase that appears in Mark 10:51. Matthew (20:29–34) and Luke (18:35–43) contain parallels to this Markan pericope. Luke shows an unnamed blind man and uses the verb ἀναβλέπω to express both the person's desire for a cure (v. 41) as well as Jesus' command affecting it (v. 42). On the other hand, Matthew (v. 33) features two unnamed blind men who request that their eyes be opened (ἀνοίγω). In the narrative, however, Matthew states that the men receive their sight by also using the verb ἀναβλέπω (v. 34).

The verb ἀναβλέπω lexically means "look up, see again, gain sight." For our purposes, we must determine whether the verb indicates a cure for a person who has always been blind, or whether a person has sight at birth, loses it, and then regains it. None of the Synoptic accounts indicate any textual problems surrounding those verses evidencing either ἀναβλέπω or ἀνοίγω, which leads to the conclusion that scribes saw no need to harmonize one version with another. They saw little difference between βλέπω and ἀναβλέπω.

Throughout Mark's Gospel, the verb ἀναβλέπω means to "look up"; the evangelist does not use it to mean "see again" or "be or become able to see." Mark uses the verb in 10:51 to describe the notion of "becoming able to see." Holding that ἀναβλέπω signifies to "look up" does not make sense in this context and so can be discounted. The question lies in choosing a translation of this verb from the two remaining possibilities: "regain one's sight," or "be or become able to see." Throughout the LXX and with minor exceptions, ἀναβλέπω connotes "to see" but always with the sense of "looking up" or "lifting up one's eyes."[19]

Other constructions of βλέπω are used within the LXX to express sight and seeing. There are two occurrences of τυφλός with βλέπω (Exod 4:11; 23:8). In both cases, blindness is contrasted with sight. Only in Isa 42:18 and 61:1, however,

---

17. Exod 4:11; Ps 146:8 [145:8 LXX]; Isa 42:16, 18; 43:8.
18. Isa 6:10; 43:8; 56:10; Jer 5:21; Ezek 12:2.
19. The minor exceptions are Tob 14:2; Tob (S) 11:8; 14:2.

do we see τυφλός used with ἀναβλέπω. The latter citation determines the reading in Mark 10:51.[20]

The second reading (Isa 61:1) is the familiar passage, "The spirit of the Lord GOD is upon me, / because the LORD has anointed me; / He has sent me to bring glad tidings to the lowly, / to heal the brokenhearted, / To proclaim liberty to the captives / and release to the prisoners." The Septuagintal version, however, concludes with the phrase τυφλοῖς ἀνάβλεψιν, which Luke features in the reading at the synagogue in Nazareth (4:18).

Mark does not quote Isaiah in the passage paralleling Luke's Nazareth synagogue scene (Mark 6:1–6), but Mark quotes the LXX versions of Isaiah elsewhere. In the opening verses of the Gospel, Mark credits Isaiah, but the verse used is actually a paraphrase of Mal 3:1. Whereas Malachi in the LXX reads ἐξαποστέλλω and ἐπιβλέψεται for "send" and "prepare," Mark uses ἀποστέλλω and κατασκευάζω. Despite the error in attestation and free use of the verse, Mark is following the LXX and not some non-Septuagintal text. Isaiah in the LXX never shows the verb ἐπιβλέπω, but it does have two instances of κατασκευάζω (40:28 and 45:7). Furthermore, Mark continues the opening verses of the Gospel by quoting Isa 40:3 LXX, which the Markan text matches word for word. Likewise, Mark 4:12 is a paraphrase of Isa 6:9–10. The evangelist may utilize the text freely, but the constructions and most of the vocabulary are directly from the LXX of Isaiah.[21]

From these similarities between the texts in the LXX and their use in Mark, we can conclude that Mark is relying on the LXX for his OT readings. The OT formed the background and lens for the earliest interpretations of Christ's life, as all four Gospels themselves attest; thus, the couplet τυφλός and ἀναβλέπω, seen only in Isa 61:1, was most likely well known among the earliest Christians. Luke, for example, writing for a predominantly Gentile community, uses the pair of words in describing Jesus' visit to the Nazareth synagogue (4:16–30). With more than relative surety, the position can be maintained that Isa 61:1 would resonate within the Jewish and Gentile audience for whom Mark was writing, and for that reason this Isaianic couplet is the reference point for the Bartimaeus story (10:46–52).

---

20. Isa 42:18 LXX uses τυφλός in the vocative and ἀναβλέπω in the imperative: "You who are deaf, listen, you who are blind, look and see!"

21. Both Mark 4:12 and Isa 6:9–10 LXX show βλέπω, ὁράω, ἀκούω, συνίημι in their constructions. The variations lie with person and voice. Similar variations appear between NT and LXX in the following: Mark 7:6–7 and Isa 29:13. Mark 7:10 and Exod 20:12; 21:15; Lev 20:9; Deut 5:16. Mark 10:7–8 and Gen 2:24. Mark 10:19 and Exod 20:12; Deut 5:16. Mark 11:9 and Ps [117] 118:26. Mark 11:17 and Isa 56:7; Jer 7:11. Mark 12:10 and Ps [117] 118:22. Mark 12:19 and Gen 38:8; Deut 25:5. Mark 12:26 and Exod 3:6, 15–16. Mark 12:29–30 and Deut 6:4–5. Mark 12:31 and Lev 19:18. Mark 12:32–33 and Lev 19:18; Deut 4:35; 6:4–5. Mark 12:36 and Ps [109] 110:1. Mark 14:62 and Dan 7:13. Mark 15:34 and Ps [21] 22:2.

Returning to the Markan use of the verb ἀναβλέπω, evidence shows that it should be translated as "regain one's sight," but with a sense that this restoration of vision is setting aright the original design of God's creation; it does not mean "to see again" with the connotation that a person had sight at one time, lost the sense of vision, and then at a later time had that vision return. Outside Saint Paul's blindness in Acts, every NT occurrence of ἀναβλέπω signifies either "to look up" or "regain, recover, restore" in the sense we have outlined.[22] Moreover, this conclusion is substantiated by the use of ἀναβλέπω in John. In the story of the man blind from birth (John 9:1–41), ἀναβλέπω has three instances: John 9:11, 15, 18. The passage states that the man was blind from birth (9:1), yet John explains the miracle by having the man say, "So I went there and washed and was able to see [ἀναβλέπω]" (John 9:11).

The healing of Bartimaeus, as with Jesus' miracles in general, is an eschatological event. As a sign of the eschaton, it restores creation to its original design and purpose, free from Satan's inroads.

## Son of David

The messianic title "Son of David" occurs only in the NT, but its origins are certainly from the OT, even though the LXX never evidences the construction. For better or for worse, when speaking of the royal descendants of King David, the phrase employed is ὁ πατὴρ αὐτοῦ Δαυιδ.[23] To be sure, υἱός signifies offspring, son, or heir, and in Mark's context of the Septuagintal term πατὴρ αὐτοῦ Δαυιδ, it connotes a Davidic descendant who has a special relationship with King David by possessing all the positive qualities and piety of that king. In biblical history, of course, the son of David is Solomon. The phrase "son of David" resurfaces in Mark a second time as Jesus teaches in the Jerusalem temple (12:35), a use that becomes more metaphorical as well as theologically refined, and its occurrence here makes Bartimaeus's call to Jesus a foreshadowing and prophetic statement.

In the NT υἱὸς Δαυιδ is nearly an exclusively Matthean phrase referring to Jesus himself.[24] The Bartimaeus pericope is the only place in Mark featuring the vocative Υἱὲ Δαυιδ.[25] However, the vocative υἱὲ τοῦ θεοῦ τοῦ ὑψίστου is

---

22. Matt 11:5; 14:19; 20:34; Mark 6:41; 7:34; 8:24; 10:51, 52; 16:4; Luke 4:18; 7:22; 9:16; 18:41, 42, 43; 19:5; 21:1; John 9:11, 15, 18; Acts 9:12, 17, 18; 22:13.

23. 1 Kgs 11:6 [8], 33; 12:[24a, not in MT and NRSV]; 15:11; 2 Kgs 14:3; 16:2; 18:3; 2 Chr 2:16; 28:1; 29:2.

24. Matthew specifically cites the term throughout his Gospel (1:1; 9:27; 12:23; 15:22; 20:30–31; 21:9, 15; 22:42, 45; but see 1:20). Mark employs it three times (10:47–48; 12:35). Luke alludes to the reference in 1:32, paraphrases it in his genealogy (3:31), shows it in 18:38–39 (the account paralleling Mark 10:46–52), as well as in 20:41, 44 (the parallel to Mark 12:35). John never features it.

25. The only other location in the NT are the parallel passages in Luke 18:38–39. See also Matt 9:27; 20:30, 31.

seen in Mark's account of the Gerasene demoniac (5:7).[26] In both these Markan occurrences, those outside the circle of Jesus' followers recognize Jesus either as a wandering preacher or wonder-worker, while the demoniac sees him as the Son of God, and Bartimaeus sees him as the Messiah promised through the Davidic line.

Nearly universal is the opinion that language stressing Jesus' Davidic line, particularly common in the Synoptics, stems from Jewish-Christian circles and therefore represents a low, primitive Christology. On the other hand, vocabulary emphasizing divine sonship, as found in the John's Gospel, reflects a high Christology, arises from among Gentile-Christians, and is a late addition. Many challenge this assumption.[27] There is a connection between a miracle-working Messiah and the royal Messiah in the expectations of first-century Jews, especially in the later rabbinic texts considering Moses' signs and wonders to have prefigured those of the "final redeemer."[28] In addition, Josephus specifically mentions that Theudas, an impostor, led masses to the Jordan River, not the wilderness.[29] The Jordan River has primary importance to both the Israelite entry into the promised land as well as the baptism of Jesus, and these two references add another dimension to the concept of the eschatological, Davidic Messiah.

By explicating Jesus' miracles within the "framework of exodus/conquest tradition, the earliest church emphasized the relevance of Jesus' miracles" to establish his status as the Messiah.[30] Moreover, the Qumran sect lends plausibility to the notion that the Righteous Teacher is the fulfillment of both Deut 18:15 and Isa 61:1, thus providing a pre-Christian foundation to claims about Jesus as the eschatological Messiah.[31] That many wished to glorify Jesus during his own lifetime also stands as evidence of a basic understanding of a divine Messiah within intertestamental Judaism.[32]

---

26. The vocative also appears in the parallel passages of the Gerasene account in Matt 8:29 and Luke 8:28.

27. Blackburn (*Theios anēr*, 248–62) makes his case and names other scholars who share his view.

28. Blackburn (ibid.) cites testimony from Josephus and Scripture, traces the idea of the "signs prophets" back to 40–70 CE, and delineates four attributes of a Moses (or Moses-Joshua) typology. These figures (1) claim to be prophets (Josephus, A.J. 20.97, 169; B.J. 2.259, 261; Deut 34:10–12), (2) lead a group of people into the wilderness (A.J. 20.97, 168, 188; B.J. 2.259, 262; 7.438; Acts 21:38), (3) promise to show signs (A.J. 20.97, 168, 170; B.J. 2.259; 7.438), and (4) work within the context of revolt from foreign domination and conquest of a land rightfully theirs (A.J. 20.98, 168–72; B.J. 2.258–63; 7.437–41; Acts 5:36; 21:38). From these readings, Blackburn concludes that it is highly likely that by the first century CE at least some Jews held Moses and the exodus events as prototypical of the eschatological, Davidic king and the salvific liberation occurring under his leadership (*Theios anēr*, 249–50). See also Joachim Jeremias, "Μωυσῆς," *TDNT* 4 (1967): 848–73.

29. Josephus, A.J. 20.97.

30. Blackburn, *Theios anēr*, 250–60.

31. Ibid., 253.

32. Blackburn (ibid., 260) uses John 2:11 as an example, even though the Johannine understanding of glory may have been different from the assumptions of earliest tradition.

The concept of the divine wonder-worker, θεῖος ἀνήρ, is not the result of Markan assimilation of Hellenistic or pagan traditions. Among Palestinian Jews of the first century were concepts and ideas of the miraculous and divine wrought by personages like Moses and Joshua, which formed the typology for messianic hope and interpretation.[33] When Bartimaeus uses the phrase "Son of David," he is acknowledging Jesus as the Messiah, the eschatological redeemer of Israel.

## The Name "Bartimaeus"

The whole central portion of Mark's Gospel (8:27–10:45) is framed by two cures, the healing of the blind man from Bethsaida (8:22–26) and the Bartimaeus story (10:46–52). In Mark's Gospel Bartimaeus is the only blind man in any Gospel given a name. Furthermore, "Bartimaeus" is the Aramaic equivalent of the Greek "Son of Timaeus," a name that is Greek and not Semitic in origin. Moreover, *Timaeus* is not an ordinary Greek name but the title of one of Plato's works. The idea that Mark makes a reference to this famous Greek work has met with various opinions.

There has been an effort to see a Hebrew connection to the name "Bartimaeus" by relying on the Hebrew root טמא, *ṭāmē'*, "unclean," to fashion a pun with the Greek τιμαῖος, meaning "honored."[34] The Markan audience would have understood that the blind one whose nation considered him unclean is, from the Christian community's perspective, "son of the most honored."[35] The problem with this reading, however, is that blindness was not considered a form of uncleanness in Jewish society, nor was it disgraceful.[36]

Although Vincent Taylor acknowledges the unknown origin of the name "Bartimaeus," he suggests that it could be a reference to Plato's character Timaeus in the work by that name.[37] Taylor thinks it more likely, however, that it is a "patronymic of Aramaic origin," and he poses a couple of reasons for this assessment.[38] He sees the proper name in verse 46 as coming from בר טמאי, "son of Timai," or even בר טמא, "son of the unclean," and he observes that Mark uses Aramaic with subsequent translations elsewhere in the Gospel.[39] Such an argument is weak in both cases.

---

33. See also ibid., 263.

34. Earle Hilgert, "The Son of Timaeus: Blindness, Sight, Ascent, Vision in Mark," *Reimagining Christian Origins* (ed. Elizabeth Castelli and Hal Taussig; Valley Forge, PA: Trinity Press International, 1996), 190–91.

35. Hilgert (ibid., 191), quoting Burton Mack.

36. The reader should remember that blindness precluded temple worship but did not ostracize one from the community. See above.

37. V. Taylor, *St. Mark*, 447.

38. Ibid., 447–48.

39. Ibid., 448.

First, "Timai" is not a proper name in biblical Hebrew or Aramaic, or at least it does not occur as such in the MT nor does it surface in a transposed form in the LXX. Second, Mark may show several Aramaisms, but in each case the evangelist does not transliterate the Aramaic by rendering it into Greek pronunciation, as is done in Mark 10:46. Furthermore, Mark always features ὅ ἐστιν to introduce the translated Greek phrase (as in 5:41; 7:11, 34; 15:34). On this basis, the supposition that "Bartimaeus" is a reference to Plato's character and work *Timaeus* is most likely the correct one, as a discussion on Timaeus's world makes clear.

## Plato's Timaeus

In the ancient world, philosophical speculation and astronomical observation were connected. The sailors, shepherds, and farmers watched the heavens as the educated classes discussed the zodiac. Plato's *Timaeus* is one work that analyzes the observable data of the stars and planets and renders scientific and philosophical conclusions based on them. The result is a compendium of the geocentric system, which formed the worldview of antiquity, a view that stayed in place up until Galileo's discoveries. In the *Timaeus*, Plato displays the cosmology of the Greco-Roman world.

Set as a dialogue between Socrates, Timaeus, Hermocrates, and Critias, the work *Timaeus* has three parts: (a) the Atlantis legend; (b) the formation of the Soul of the World, including the doctrine of elements and the theory of matter and sense objects; and (c) the making of the human soul and body.[40] For our purposes, the last two sections are the most pertinent. They provide the ancient anthropology dealing with the creation of the universe and the human being's place within it. Plato's *Timaeus* not only furnishes a record of mathematical and astronomical discoveries; it also sees in these discoveries the laws that determine human souls and emotions. According to Plato, the well-being of the individual lies in "conforming to the universal order, the rhythmical step of the cosmos, and the tune of the celestial harmonies."[41] Examples from the work make this point clearer.

Critias claims that Timaeus, the "best astronomer," is to begin speaking about the origin of the cosmos and is to end with the generation of humankind.[42] Since Timaeus bases his science on observing the heavens, right from the start of the dialogue Plato establishes the link between the celestial and human order. To be sure, he is not the only one in the ancient world to do so. The creation stories in Genesis are similar in this regard, and by extension so are the Egyptian and

---

40. R. G. Bury, trans., *Plato*, vol. 9, *Timaeus, Critias, Cleitophon, Menexenus, Epistles* (LCL; Cambridge, MA: Harvard University Press, 1989), 4.

41. Ibid., 14.

42. Plato, *Timaeus* 27a (LCL 9:46).

Babylonian myths. The point is that the biblical account is *not* unique in seeing a connection between the creation of the cosmos and humankind.

In his task Timaeus relies heavily on mathematics, which he explains in full if sometimes confusing detail. In his description of the "outer revolution of the same and the inner revolution of the other," Timaeus speaks of their forming a great cross (χι) with the arms of each bent backward to form two circles, one within the other. Each of these circles has its own revolution running contrary to each other. The outer circle (the revolution of the same) is the celestial equator, and the inner circle (the revolution of the other) is the ecliptic. On the inner circle are set what were then considered the seven planets: the Sun, Venus, Mercury, the Moon, Mars, Jupiter, and Saturn.[43] Furthermore, God (ὁ θεός) gave each planet (variously called a "wandering star" within the text) its own orbit.[44] In this scheme, the Earth, considered not a planet but the "first and eldest of the gods," stands at the center of the universe.[45] This universe, affected by the balance of the inner and outer revolutions, becomes an "eternal living creature" (ζῷον ἀίδιον ὄν). As a living creature, the universe has generative capacity, but it is unable to hold in its entirety everything that it generates. The Father, understood as the uncaused cause, therefore made a moveable image of Eternity, which is called "time."[46]

Timaeus observes that the movement of all the "wandering stars," or planets — as differentiated from all the "fixed stars," meaning stars as science understands them today — determine human events, even though he maintains that, despite many attempts at doing so, it is impossible to read these portents.[47] The terms Plato uses to describe these movements underscore the importance of the intersections of these orbits: χορείας δὲ τούτων αὐτῶν καὶ παραβολὰς ἀλλήλων.[48] These "dances" and "crossings" demonstrate an organized pattern that caused changes, both good and ill, to occur. We should focus our attention on the formation of a cross that many heavenly bodies, which Timaeus calls "gods,"[49] made in their migration, particularly that of the celestial equator and the ecliptic.

At this point in the *Timaeus*, Plato enters into a discourse on the senses, beginning with vision. Vision is the "cause of the greatest benefit to us."[50] Not only is vision responsible for giving the human race the ability to count and to

---

43. Ibid., 36b, c–d (9:68–72).
44. Ibid., 38c–d (9:78).
45. Ibid., 40b–c (9:84). Bury, the translator, observes the assumption that the earth's potential motion is equal and opposite to that of the universe, thereby neutralizing the universe's movement so that the earth remains at rest (9:85).
46. Ibid., 37d–e (9:74–76).
47. Ibid., 40a–d (9:84–86).
48. Ibid., 40c (9:84).
49. Ibid., 41a (9:86).
50. Ibid., 47a (9:107).

mark time, but it has also given them the ability to probe the nature of the universe, which in turn leads to philosophy, through which "no greater boon ever has come or will come by divine bestowal unto the race of mortals."[51] These noble words of Plato precede what for him is the ultimate curse of blindness: ὧν ὁ μὴ φιλόσοφος τυφλωθεὶς ὀδυρόμενος ἂν θρηνοῖ μάτην;[52] "The nonphilosopher being a blind person may weep vainly in grief."[53] Plato concludes this discourse by stating that in observation of the heavenly revolutions, one observes reason at work, and this reason can be imitated to establish reason within the individual.[54] Such a gift of reason, of course, leads to philosophy, which for Plato is the highest good. The inability to see prevents one from achieving or approaching the good, a curse indeed.

Yet, the "son of Timaeus" (Mark 10:46) is blind and therefore a nonphilosopher, weeping vainly in grief. When healed of his blindness, he does not gaze at the stars but follows Jesus to the cross. Rather than the celestial equator intersecting with the ecliptic, the cross becomes a seeming instrument of death that yields to life. The cross with the crucified Jesus truly becomes then an "eternal living creature," with true generative capacity. It is greater than the universe and contains the universe; it is able to hold everything it generates.

It is tempting to wonder whether the focus on the cross in the text of Mark's Gospel as well as Paul's emphasis on it throughout his writings is somehow a response to the Platonic claim that salvation lay at the intersection of the celestial equator and the ecliptic. In the *Timaeus*, this junction tethers these two essential orbits, which hold together life while engendering it. Early statues of Mithras depict this cross superimposed on his body. Likewise, in the Christian tradition the cross of Christ is the source of eternal life. The first known artistic representation of the crucified Christ is found on the wooden doors of the Basilica of Santa Sabina in Rome. It dates from 422–432, the same period that saw the rise of many mithraea in Rome.

## *The Cross*

In the introduction I state that Mark's Gospel has an inherent participation-ist theology, certainly augmented by Paul and probably introduced by him. The Markan theme of discipleship is akin to the Pauline notion of participation in Christ. So, does Paul augment Markan teachings on discipleship/participation, or does he introduce them? Here I suggest that we must break the question down

---

51. Ibid., 47b (9:107).
52. Ibid., 47b (9:106).
53. Ibid.; translation mine.
54. Ibid., 47b–c (9:106–108).

into two components: the make-up of the Jewish-Christian community in Rome, and Paul's understanding of Christ's crucifixion.

By the time Claudius comes to power in 41 CE, the Jewish-Christian community in Rome suffers a rift and expels the Jews for reasons associated with civil disturbances arising over the person of "Chrestus," or Christ. This period is nearly twenty years before Paul enters the capital. The Letter to the Galatians is the earliest record we have of Paul's tangling with the Judaizers, whether one goes by the earlier or later dating of the piece.[55] In either case, Claudius's expulsion of the Jews was precipitated by riots revolving around the Christ event. Judaizers, however, disturbed the harmony among Gentile Christians, and they arrive on the scene in the eastern regions (Antioch and Asia Minor) some four to five years after Claudius's edict (ca. 49). The Letter to the Romans does not evidence the high tension surrounding issues of the Mosaic law vis-à-vis baptism in Christ found in such places as Galatia, Colossae, or Corinth. Furthermore, even if Judaizers ever made it to Rome, they would have found few, if any, Jews there until after Claudias' death in 54, when they were allowed to return to Rome. By the time Paul wrote Romans (ca. 54–58), a more chastened and quieter Jewish population would have been residing in Rome, and any Judaizers would have been more circumspect in their preaching. Paul would not have been pressed to stress in Rome the modality of Jesus' death; he could have made the same point about salvation through Christ's cross in another way. This leads to the second component of the question.

Paul uses the verb "crucify" only once in Romans (6:6) Actually, in this case it is a compound verb, an indicative passive meaning "to be crucified together with someone else" (συσταυρόομαι), and it refers to the baptized being crucified with Christ. The context explains that Christians are crucified with Christ in death in order to rise with him in life; it is a participationist theology. Paul, similar to the view of the cosmos outlined in Plato's *Timaeus*, saw the world as animate. Here I suggest that Paul augments the discipleship/participationist theology in Mark by underscoring the cross, a cross that for the Gentiles would have strongly echoed with their views of the cosmos as they understood it from the prevailing and accepted thought of the universe, as based on the *Timaeus*. In this vein, then, Paul could uncompromisingly present his most deeply held conviction of the necessity of crucifixion as the modality of Jesus' death. Doing so need not have radically shifted the Jewish tradition behind Mark's Gospel. Yet for the Gentile community in Rome it presented a way in which they could at least conceptually

---

55. The dating hinges on to whom Paul wrote in Galatians. If the recipients were those living in the north around Ancyra, the letter was probably written around 54–55 CE. If Paul on the other hand was directing the epistle to the cities of southern Galatia (where Acts has him preaching on his missionary journeys), the dating would be about 48–50.

appropriate the cross of Christ as the means of salvation, by showing how disciples become one with the Lord of the universe. It is this cosmic significance of the cross and the participation in the life of the cosmos through Christ that Paul introduces to the Christian community in Rome.

## Timaeus and Bartimaeus

In Plato's *Timaeus*, Critias describes Timaeus as "our best astronomer... [who] has made it his special task to learn about the nature of the Universe" (27a).[56] Timaeus sees the heavens, recognizes the stars, and explains the cosmos to Socrates in the company of Critias and Hermocrates. He observes a universe that is good, whole, and perfect. The cosmos that Timaeus sees is much different from the world that Mark describes in his Gospel; indeed, the world in Mark's Gospel, nearly in antithesis to Timaeus's world, is the lot of nearly all humankind. In Mark's world are physical suffering, demonic possession, and death.

The terms "demon" or "demons" are instanced fifteen times within Mark's Gospel, and the settings are often associated with illness or physical disability.[57] People suffer paralysis (2:3–12), deafness, and muteness (7:32, 37; 9:25). Moreover, Satan is depicted as having a strong grip on the world (1:13; 3:23, 26; 4:15; 8:33). What we see is a creation filled with suffering tied with death, a point Timaeus avoids (Plato, *Tim.* 35–41).[58] Where Timaeus speaks about evil, it is usually in the context of a man who does not live his life well; at death he is changed into "some bestial form after the similitude of his own nature" (42C).[59] What Timaeus does not address is the evil that threatens the good of the created world, and the good who suffer because of it.

With the use of the name "Bartimaeus" in 10:46, Mark questions Timaeus's vision. As a son, Bartimaeus is the heir of Plato's character Timaeus, blind and crying out in lament. It seems that Mark is writing a mimesis of Plato.[60] As a mimesis, Bartimaeus calls into question the moral order of Timaeus's universe, and in so doing acts as the voice for suffering, lost, and perishing humankind. Jesus, however, does not leave Bartimaeus wallowing in despair. Though physically blind, Bartimaeus has spiritual insight that causes him to call out for mercy from the Son of David (10:47–48), and the Son of David grants it (10:52).

---

56. Bury, *Plato*, LCL 9:47.
57. Mark 1:32, 34, 39; 3:15, 22; 5:15–16, 18; 6:13; 7:26, 29, 30; 9:38; 16:9, 17.
58. Bury, *Plato*, LCL 9:64–91.
59. Ibid., 9:93.
60. See Gordon Lathrop, "Biblical and Liturgical Reorientation in the World," *Worship* 77, no. 1 (January 2003): 2–22.

Although all three Synoptics relate a version of this story, only Mark includes the detail of Bartimaeus casting off the cloak in 10:50.[61] This detail has puzzled some exegetes. One interpretation holds that the blind beggar would not be wearing the garment; rather, he would have it spread on the ground in front of him in order to collect the alms people would drop. His action of tossing it aside, therefore, would be more dramatic and decisive.[62] Another tries to connect it to the youth who runs away naked at the arrest.[63]

The symbolism of Bartimaeus's cloak goes deeper than either of these suggestions. "Cloak" (ἱμάτιον, singular) occurs five times in Mark.[64] With the exception of references to touching Jesus' cloak (5:27; 6:56), the use of the term "cloak" signifies an old way of life that should be abandoned. In Mark 2:21, Jesus advises that mending an old cloak with a new patch is counterproductive. Likewise, turning back to retrieve one's cloak could bring death (13:16). Cloaks wrap and protect, but they also hinder sight and hamper movement. Bartimaeus casts off his cloak for precisely that reason; it represents the old way of seeing reality and responding to it. By throwing off his cloak, Bartimaeus makes a radical break with his past.[65] On this score, throwing off the cloak has resonance with the baptismal liturgy.

From Mark's presentation of the cure of Bartimaeus, it is unclear whether Bartimaeus is Jewish. He is sitting along the road in the Jewish city of Jericho; yet as an oasis serving as a junction for various trade routes, Jericho would have Gentiles present at any given time. Above all, his calling out to Jesus with the title Υἱὲ Δαυίδ is itself a likely indication that Bartimaeus is Jewish. If in every other circumstance this blind man appears to be Jewish, why does Mark give him the Hellenized name Bartimaeus?

One possibility is that Bartimaeus's non-Semitic name, utilizing the decidedly Greek legend and archetype of Timaeus, is highly indicative that the evangelist wants to portray this beggar as a Greek. The Aramaic prefix *bar*, however, is followed by the explanation in Greek that this man is the son of Timaeus (10:46), thereby suggesting the possibility that he is Jewish and that the evangelist wishes to explain his identity to a Greek audience. A third possibility, which I feel is most likely, is that Mark is appealing to Jews who feel so comfortable in their Hellenized world that they look to Greek philosophy to complement their Jewish belief. In so doing, he is also appealing to a non-Jewish audience. In other words, by carefully establishing the identity of the blind man in two languages, Mark is

61. See Matt 20:29–34 and Luke 18:35–43.
62. V. Taylor, *St. Mark*, 449.
63. Gordon Lathrop, *Holy Ground: A Liturgical Cosmology* (Minneapolis: Fortress, 2003), 10–11.
64. Mark 2:21; 5:27; 6:56; 10:50; 13:16.
65. See R. Alan Culpepper, "Why Mention the Garment?" *JBL* 101, no. 1 (March 1982): 131–32.

insisting, and leaving little room for doubt, that the beggar is indeed the son of Timaeus. Mark wants to tell both Jews and Gentiles who would seek salvation in a Greek cosmology that they are looking in the wrong place.

This conclusion fits well within the Markan narrative. In the story of the Syro-phoenician woman (7:24–30), Mark uses the proper term for a "Greek" woman, Ἑλληνίς, to describe her ethnic background (7:26). By this choice of vocabu-lary, Mark delineates Greeks from other non-Jews, to whom he refers as ἔθνος.[66] A close reading shows that the Greek, Syrophoenician woman's daughter, and therefore the woman herself, are saved through faith in Christ (7:29), just as the Greek-named Bartimaeus, through his faith, is healed of blindness. In those passages where Mark uses ἔθνος, salvation for the non-Jews is not excluded, but there is no single or particular person involved in the narrative (Mark 10:33, 42; 11:17; 13:8, 10). It appears, therefore, that by providing examples of two specif-ically Greek personages who demonstrate faith in Jesus, as opposed to a more general treatment of non-Jews, Mark is opening the way for Gentiles to find the hope of salvation in the Jewish Jesus.

Mark uses Bartimaeus, now cured of blindness, not only as an example of a faithful call to discipleship; in addition, by employing such a crucial name and depicting the removal of the cloak, the evangelist also portrays a cosmic shift affected by Christ. The moral universe described by Plato's Timaeus has collapsed. The Bartimaeus story, coupled with the use of the verb σχίζω in the baptism (1:9–11) and death (15:33–39), describes a whole new world coming into existence with Christ. Furthermore, the crucial verb ἀκολουθέω in 10:52 makes Bartimaeus a disciple. Mark stresses that immediately after Jesus commands, "Go your way; your faith has saved you," Bartimaeus looks up and follows him as the scene shifts to the entry into Jerusalem, the city of Jesus' passion, death, and resurrection. In Mark's Gospel, Bartimaeus becomes the disciple who is willing to drink from the cup from which Jesus drinks and to be baptized with the baptism with which he is baptized (10:38–39).

## Discipleship

The setting of the Bartimaeus pericope within the Markan narrative is also im-portant. Bartimaeus sits along the road in Jericho, the town where Jesus and his band will turn west and begin the ascent to Jerusalem. The earthly ministry is nearing completion, and in fact, the next scene is the triumphant entry into Jeru-salem. We read of Bartimaeus: "Immediately [he] received his sight and followed

---

66. See Mark 10:33, 42; 11:17; 13:8, 10.

[ἀκολουθέω) him on the way" (10:52). Bartimaeus becomes a disciple and follows Jesus to his passion and death, and by extension, his resurrection.[67]

Bartimaeus has always been blind, and as such, he represents the old creation, the creation described by Timaeus. Now that Jesus is passing by, he has the opportunity to have his sight repaired, restored to the order that God originally had designed for the now-fallen cosmos. Bartimaeus participates in this new creation by becoming a disciple and following Jesus to the cross.[68] In addition to "follow, accompany," the Greek verb ἀκολουθέω signifies "to be a disciple." Mark uses the various meanings interchangeably, and often the verb implies all of them simultaneously, as it does in 10:52.

The miracle stories in Mark's Gospel are concentrated within the first eight chapters. Starting with Peter's declaration at Caesarea Philippi (8:27–33), the evangelist switches to the teaching ministry, which is focused on the death and resurrection.[69] The two exceptions to this division are the healing of the possessed boy (9:14–29) and this Bartimaeus passage. These two pericopes inform each other in developing Mark's Christology. Indeed, one should be cautious in viewing the story of Bartimaeus solely as an example of discipleship; hence, we see the importance of Bartimaeus's call to Jesus, "Son of David," a title that appears only here (10:47). More than an account of discipleship, the Bartimaeus story is the place in which both the christological image of Jesus and the response to discipleship converge; Christology and discipleship, then, are intimately related.[70] The preceding miracles and healings form the context for the confession. The demands and destiny of discipleship (suffering and death) are presented to the disciples, and the disciple Peter rejects them. In the Bartimaeus story, on the other hand, Jesus' ministry is declared to be Son-of-David activity, a designation that Jesus accepts. Bartimaeus indicates not only that he has a proper understanding of Jesus, but also by his action of following Jesus he demonstrates his willingness to face consequences in Jerusalem, thus becoming a model of discipleship. Mark also uses this interpretation of discipleship to develop his Christology.

---

67. Johnson ("Bartimaeus," 198–204) makes this point as well.

68. Humphrey (*Risen!* 97–99) contrasts Bartimaeus to the blind man in 8:22–26, whose sight returns only in stages, as with the disciples, who have difficulty accepting the demands of discipleship and only come to it gradually. In this sense, 10:46–52 looks "backwards to the 'blindness' of the disciples, and . . . forward . . . to Jesus' passion and death."

69. See Robbins, "Healing," 225.

70. See John R. Donahue, *Are You the Christ? The Trial Narrative in the Gospel of Mark* (SBLDS 10; Missoula, MT: Society of Biblical Literature, 1973), who elaborates this point by indicating that discipleship is often linked to Jesus on his ὁδός (way) "to Jerusalem and his death" (211–12). Similarly, Robbins, "Healing," views the confession at Caesarea Philippi (8:27–33) as the Markan parallel to the Bartimaeus pericope (227).

## Bartimaeus and Markan Christology

Jesus enters Jerusalem with the crowd shouting, "Blessed is the kingdom of our father David that is to come" (Mark 11:10).[71] The affirmation of Davidic sonship, however, has ramifications going beyond the Jewish understanding of the concept and on to a movement toward the Gentile world. Once inside Jerusalem, Jesus cleanses the temple (Mark 11:15–19). While this dramatic action can be interpreted as Jesus preparing the outer court to provide for Gentile worship (11:17), it could also have a sole importance for some within the Jewish community who could have viewed this action as part of the expectation associated with the eschatological Davidic descendant.[72] Moreover, the parable of the Wicked Tenants (Mark 12:1–12) introduces the idea that, since King David made Jerusalem the center of Israel after wresting its control from the Jebusites, the Son of David has the authority to change the composition of both leaders and the people. In addition, healing was associated with the Son of David, and Mark uses "Son of David" only in a healing story (10:46–52)[73] ; thus, the Bartimaeus story serves as a link between Jesus' healing activity in Mark 1–10 and the Davidic traditions surrounding Jesus in Jerusalem. Jesus' authority is not only from Davidic, human origin, but also from heaven (Mark 1:11; 9:7). We can conclude, therefore, that Mark sees the Son of David as the Son of God, and the healing of Bartimaeus, undergirded by Mark 11:27–33 and 12:1–12, connects the two theological points.

## Précis

The study of the Bartimaeus pericope concentrates on four terms: "blindness," "Son of David," "see again," and "follow."

In the ancient world, curing blindness is a popular healing story in both Gentile and Jewish circles. In the latter, for the blind to have their sight restored would be interpreted as a sign of the eschaton. The prophetic tradition often presents those suffering physical blindness as having spiritual insight and vice versa. The terms τυφλός and ἀναβλέπω otherwise appear as a couplet only in Isa 61:1 LXX, the referent for the Bartimaeus story. When Jesus heals Bartimaeus's sight, he restores the original design of God's creation as well as signals the eschaton.

The term "Son of David" occurs only in the NT but draws on a long tradition in which miracle working is seen as a sign of the royal Messiah. When Bartimaeus

---

71. Robbins, "Healing," observes that at this point the crowd display their Davidic expectations while indirectly asserting the Davidic sonship of Jesus. The Bartimaeus story is crucial in developing the term "Son of David" to become "Christian in content" (241–42).

72. Robbins ("Healing," 241) cites Isa 11:10 LXX; *T. Sim.* 7:1b–2; *T. Jud.* 24:5b.

73. 1 Sam 16:23; 18:10; 19:9.

uses the title "Son of David," he is acknowledging Jesus as both the Messiah and the eschatological redeemer of Israel.

"Bartimaeus" is a name meant to recall for the reader Plato's *Timaeus*, to which it stands opposed. This name would resonate with both Greeks and Hellenized Jews. Bartimaeus becomes a disciple, and his alacrity in doing so, symbolized by tossing off his cloak and following Jesus, takes on baptismal imagery. As a disciple, Bartimaeus connects the Son of David to the Son of God.

## Chapter 8

# Death and Resurrection of Jesus (Mark 15:33–16:8)

The death of Jesus is the second pillar supporting Mark's cosmology. The point of contact between these verses and those at the baptism (1:9–11) is the Greek verb σχίζω, which appears in Mark only at these two places. If the rending of the heavens at the baptism symbolizes God's reaching down to creation, the rending of the temple veil symbolizes the effect of creation's reply. That effect is access between the earthly and heavenly realities made possible by Jesus' ministry, passion, death, and resurrection.

## The Death Cry (Mark 15:34, 37–38)

[34]And at three o'clock Jesus cried out in a loud voice, "*Eloi, Eloi, lema sabachthani?*" which is translated, "My God, my God, why have you forsaken me?" . . .

[37]Jesus gave a loud cry and breathed his last. [38]The veil of the sanctuary was torn in two from top to bottom.

Several questions arise from the verses describing Jesus' death as well as the description of the tearing of the temple veil. The first centers on the death cry. In a study investigating the similarities and differences between the Aramaic and Hebrew languages, Harald Sahlin[1] suggests that the tradition behind the last words of Christ reflects confusion between what Christ might have said and what bystanders probably heard. Sahlin retranslates into Aramaic what the bystanders thought they heard: '*Ēlîâ tā*', "Elijah, come!"[2] He suggests that Jesus actually cries out in Hebrew: '*Ēlî* '*attâ*, "My God, are you!" In this case, the misunderstanding is perfectly comprehensible since '*Ēlî* '*attâ* and '*Ēlîâ tā*' sound the same.[3] Sahlin reports that the phrase '*Ēlî* '*attâ*, in addition to occurring in Isa 44:17, also appears

---

1. Harald Sahlin, "Mk 15,34," *Bib* 33 (1952): 62–66.
2. In Aramaic, *tā*' (or '*ĕtā*') is the imperative of '*ātā*', "to come," as in the expression *Marana tha* (1 Cor 16:22).
3. Sahlin, "Mk 15,34," 63–64.

in Pss 22:10 [11]; 63:1 [2]; 118:28; and 140:6 [7].[4] Indeed, Ps 22:10 [11] reads, "From my mother's womb, my God, are you." Furthermore, Ps 31:14 [15] has, "But I count on you, Lord; I say: My God, are you."[5]

Following the cry is the rending of the temple veil. The verb σχίζω (Mark 15:38) harks back to the baptism (1:10–11), its only other occurrence, where three actions surface. The first is that the heavens are rent open (σχίζω, pass. ptc.); the second is that the Spirit descends; and the third is that the voice from the heavens speaks, "You are my beloved Son; with you I am well pleased." The baptism, in turn, is connected to the transfiguration (9:2–10) by a voice from a cloud, "This is my beloved Son. Listen to him" (9:7). Each of these pericopes — baptism, transfiguration, and death — grounds Mark's overarching theology, a theology that shows a divine communication with creation. Unlike the first two occasions, however, the third divine communication does not come from the heavens to creation; instead, it is a response of creation to the divine in the heavens. This point can be developed further by an examination of the three pericopes: the baptism, transfiguration, and the death.

## The Baptism (Mark 1:9–11)

[9]It happened in those days that Jesus came from Nazareth of Galilee and was baptized in the Jordan by John. [10]On coming up out of the water he saw the heavens being torn open and the Spirit, like a dove, descending upon him. [11]And a voice came from the heavens, "You are my beloved Son; with you I am well pleased."

## The Transfiguration (Mark 9:7)

[7]Then a cloud came, casting a shadow over them; then from the cloud came a voice, "This is my beloved Son. Listen to him."

Whereas the account of the baptism speaks about the Spirit coming to Jesus as a dove, with a voice from heaven speaking to him, the transfiguration passage describes a cloud overshadowing or covering Jesus, Peter, James, and John. There is also a voice "from the cloud" in the third person declaring Jesus' identity along

---

4. Ibid., 64.
5. Ibid., 64n1. See Thorleif Boman, "Das letzte Wort Jesu," in *ST* 17 (1963): 103–19, who claims that the Lukan and Johannine accounts are also based on 'Ēli' āttâ. Boman connects the phrase "My God, are you," found in Ps 31:14 [15], with the Luke's paraphrase of Ps 31:5 [6], "Father, into your hands I commend my spirit" (Luke 23:46). Likewise, Boman holds that Ps 63:1 [2], "You are my God; ... for you my soul thirsts," forms the literary and theological background for the Johannine account of Jesus' cry "I thirst" (19:28).

with a second-person plural imperative, "Listen to him" (9:7). Any similarity with
the baptism is limited to the voice, but even here, the parallel is not exact. In
the baptism the statement is in the second person, leading to the conclusion that
only Jesus hears it. In the transfiguration the voice is speaking to Jesus and the
others, and they all hear the message. In each case, however, the voice asserts
Jesus' divine sonship: in the former, to Jesus alone; and in the latter, to Jesus and
three disciples.

## The Death (Mark 15:34, 37–38)

[34]And at three o'clock Jesus cried out in a loud voice, "*Eloi, Eloi, lema
sabachthani?*" which is translated, "My God, my God, why have you forsaken
me?"...[6]

[37]Jesus gave a loud cry and breathed his last. [38]The veil of the sanctuary
was torn in two from top to bottom.

When compared to the baptism and the transfiguration, the single and most
obvious difference between this scene and the previous two is that here the voice
comes before the curtain is torn, while at the baptism it sounds after the heavens
are rent. Moreover, the account of the transfiguration does not use the verb
σχίζω. Since the temple is the place where God resides on earth, the rending of
the curtain parallels the splitting of the heavens at the baptism. If the heavens
are torn at the baptism, leading into the descent of the Spirit and proclamation
of the divine voice, the process is reversed at the death. Jesus cries out from the
cross, gives up his spirit (ἐξέπνευσεν), and the temple curtain is torn.

Interpreting the death of Jesus must incorporate everything from the baptism
through the earthly ministry, for the death and resurrection are the culmination
of his earthly life. Jesus has been engaged in a battle with Satan for control over
the cosmos. That death on the cross is the climax of that battle, and the two
Markan uses of σχίζω along with their respective contexts show the significance
of Jesus' ministry and death. This significance would be particularly evident within
the understanding of the universe shared by the ancients.

## Heaven and the Heavens

The traditional OT construct of the universe was essentially geocentric; the earth
was at the center of Yahweh's creation. Many scholars have described and illus-
trated the biblical concept, but among all of them, there are certain, common

---

6. The textual tradition of the last words of Jesus is complex. See Michael Patella, *The Death of
Jesus* (CahRB 43; Paris: J. Gabalda, 1999), 85–86.

characteristics.[7] The earth is a large ball suspended in the heavens. The outer shell of this ball is called the firmament. Within the firmament are the fields, rivers, seas, and mountains — the living space for humans, birds, fish, and animals. The sun, moon, stars, and planets are also encased within the ball but above the earth. Below the ground but still encased within the firmament lies the underworld, or in Hebrew, Sheol. Waters surround the whole firmament, and floodgates at the top of the firmament let in rain or other precipitation. Above and beyond these waters is Yahweh's throne, unseen by human eye, although in a prophetic or dreamlike state the heavenly realm became visible.[8] This idea forms the basic outline of the universe, and several biblical passages reflect it to a greater or lesser degree.[9] The salient point is that God lives above, in the highest heaven, while humankind dwells on the earth below; God is inaccessible, and there is no way for humans to bridge the gap.[10]

The yawning divide separating the human and divine realms does not prevent prophets from calling upon God to come down and visit his people, but no individual has the temerity to suppose that oneself can rise to Yahweh's throne in the heavens (Isa 64:1 [63:19]). Humans on earth could approach the divine presence only in the temple. The temple provided a place where God could manifest himself, but God does not dwell there.[11] Although Ezekiel sees visions of God, the divine passive verb (ἀνοίγω) indicates that the initiative for the rending of the heavens comes from God (1:1 LXX).

The OT mentions only two individuals who traverse the chasm between earth and the heavens above the firmament. Elijah, in the midst of a whirlwind, is assumed into heaven by a flaming chariot and horses (2 Kgs 2:11), and in Genesis, God simply takes Enoch up (5:24). Moses and select elders behold God on Mount Sinai, but they all return down the mountain (Exod 24:9–11), unlike Enoch or Elijah who are assumed up and never seen again. Sirach, a later work, explains: "Enoch walked with the LORD and was taken up, / that succeeding generations might learn by his example" (44:16). "Few on earth have been made the equal of Enoch, for he was taken up bodily" (49:14). In both these cases, however, the

---

7. See J. Edward Wright, *The Early History of Heaven* (New York: Oxford University Press, 2000), 87–109, who provides a scholarly overview of Persian and Hellenistic concepts of heaven and supplies artistic sketches.
8. Wright (ibid., 95) makes the point that Yahweh's consort, Asherah, as well as Baal may also have been part of the heavenly realm. Even in this case, the heavenly throne was still inaccessible to human beings. See Isa 6; Ezek 1; Dan 7.
9. In addition to the two creation accounts in Gen 1–2, see Gen 49:22–26; Deut 10:14; 33:26; Judg 5:20; 2 Sam 22:8–16; Pss [103 LXX] 104; 148; 150:1–2; Sir 16:16; Isa 65:17; Jer 51:15.
10. Gen 28:10–17; Deut 26:15; 1 Kgs 8:27, 30, 39, 43, 49; 2 Kgs 19:15; 2 Chr 2:5–6; 6:18, 30, 33, 39; Pss 8:1 [2 LXX]; [18:2] 19:1; [28] 29:10; [67] 68:34; [79:2] 80:1; [98] 99:1; [113:24] 115:16; Prov 8:27; 30:4; Eccl 5:[1] 2; Isa 37:16; 40:22; Lam 5:19.
11. See 2 Sam 22:7–11; 1 Kgs 9:1–7; Jer 7:3–7.

initiative is solely God's. Neither Enoch nor Elijah leap up to God on his own, and according to this cosmology, they could not do so. Another late (deutero-canonical) OT writing, Wisdom of Solomon, begins to develop the point that God rewards a person for living righteously.

Wisdom was composed in Greek and appears in the LXX. Along with its Greek language, it reflects patterns of Greek thought and philosophy. Most of the work offers a comparison between the life of the righteous and that of the ungodly, and it features the phrase ἡμέρα διαγνώσεως (Wis 3:18), which can be translated as "the day of decision, scrutiny, judgment." Although there are many OT references to Yahweh's judgment, both on the pagan nations as well as on a disobedient Israel, only Wisdom and the pseudepigraphic *Psalms of Solomon* speak of God's judgment between the righteous and the unrighteous, and both appear under the Hellenistic cultural sway.[12] When Jewish thought encounters the Hellenistic world, the concept of immortality, at least for the righteous, enters Jewish tradition.[13]

A belief in a heavenly reward for the righteous can be seen in such passages as Eccl 3:17–21 and Dan 12:1–3, which demonstrate an influence from both Persian and Hellenistic cultures. In these two passages we can see a merging of OT notions of the heavens with the Greek idea of the immortality of the soul. Ascent to heaven is impossible in this life, but after death a righteous individual could perhaps go beyond the firmament and into the divine realm of the heavens above.

Part of the Greek legacy in cosmology was the idea of multiple heavens. While the Greeks, especially through their mathematics, were making great strides in astronomy, especially in tracing the orbits of the moon and the planets and the spherical nature of heavenly bodies, the Persians also were studying the skies. Indeed, the Persians invented the zodiac and horoscope. Unlike the Greeks and Romans, who reckoned that the universe was composed of seven levels of the heavens, the Persians believed there were three. These Mediterranean and Mesopotamian civilizations shared the idea, however, that a good person's soul ascended through each heavenly sphere in order to reach its place of origin. Scholars see the confluence of Greco-Roman and Persian thought gaining great popularity in Rome in the form of astral religions from about 200 BCE onward.[14] Many of these astral religions took shape as mystery cults and were the basis of most gnostic belief systems, of which the Mithras cult was the most popular.

Speculation on the nature of the afterlife also operated on another level of Greek thought. While the Greek astronomers and mathematicians, with the help

---

12. *Psalms of Solomon* (e.g., 15:12), unlike Wis 3:18, uses ἡμέρα κρίσεως.

13. See also Jan Nelis, "God and Heaven in the Old Testament," in *Heaven* (ed. Bas van Iersel and Edward Schillebeeckx; Concilium: Religion in the Seventies; New York: Seabury, 1979), 22–33.

14. Wright, *History*, 109.

of Persian thought, were calculating the composition and structure of the universe, Greek myth and literature offered a parallel but not always distinct manner of dealing with life after death. Over time, these two views merged.

## Markan Picture

Were it not for the verb σχίζω, the portrayal of Jesus dying on the cross followed by the tearing of the temple curtain would lead to a darkly apocalyptic interpretation devoid of any eschatological hope. Such a depiction would consequently show an even greater chasm between God in the heavens and humans on earth. The word σχίζω, however, balances the death with the baptism. In addition, the verb σχίζω (Mark 1:10; 15:38), and the voice from heaven (Mark 1:11; 9:7), along with the cry from the cross (15:34) — these all tie together the baptism, transfiguration, and the death. Furthermore, by their immediate contexts within Mark's Gospel, each of these events includes Jesus' whole mission.[15]

The Father calls out to the Son at 1:11, and the Son responds from the cross at 15:34. The voice from the cloud at the transfiguration (9:7) serves to manifest to the disciples what the Father states to Jesus at the baptism. At Jesus' arrest and passion, everyone forsakes him. In Mark 15:34, Jesus is completely abandoned as he enters the dark night of death alone. Jesus' cry from the cross, the cry of all creation to the Creator, is a despairing lament. The sanctuary veil is torn from top to bottom in 15:38. One interpretation of this ripping is that Mark signals to the reader that, with Jesus' death, all now have access to God. A better way of looking at it, however, is that, with Jesus' death, God no longer manifests himself in the temple. If one wishes to see God, one must look to the cross. There is an eschatological thrust to the whole Markan picture that ultimately is hopeful and optimistic: Satan is defeated, and all the cosmos is united with its creator. This fortunate resolution does not come easily. The Son of God dies on the cross, but the cross is not the final answer; the resurrection is.

## Markan Resurrection Account (16:1–8)

The being at the tomb is a young man (νεανίσκος, 16:5). The only other citation of this term in the Markan Gospel is at the arrest, where Mark includes a puzzling

---

15. The preaching of John the Baptist (1:1–8) precedes Jesus' baptism, and the baptism itself (1:9–11) is followed by the desert temptation (1:12–13) and the beginnings of Jesus' ministry (1:14–15). The transfiguration (9:2–8) is set between the first passion prediction and rebuke to Peter (8:31–33) and an expulsion (9:14–29) as well as the second passion prediction (9:30–32). The passion narrative begins after the explanation of true discipleship (10:38–39, 42–45) and the healing of Bartimaeus (10:46–52).

verse describing the naked young man who flees the scene (14:51–52). One interpretation of the scene is that this individual is the same person at the tomb now. Moreover, he has a link extending back to Bartimaeus, whose name never appears again in the Markan Gospel.[16]

That Bartimaeus, the unquestioning disciple, casts off his cloak (10:50) before coming to Jesus underscores the parallel this pericope has with the young man running naked in 14:51–52. Having the same youth sitting at the tomb makes him a model of the newly baptized, someone who has been "immersed in the death of Jesus in order to be clothed in his life" and made a witness of the resurrection.[17] In this understanding, there is a gradual but perceptible progression of the connection. In 10:50 Bartimaeus throws off his cloak (ἱμάτιον), and in 14:51–52 the young man (νεανίσκος) flees without a linen cloth (σινδών). At his burial, Jesus is wrapped in a linen cloth (σινδών, 15:46), while at the tomb announcing Jesus' resurrection to the women is a young man (νεανίσκος) dressed in a long robe (στολή, 16:5). The reprise of the linen cloth at the burial of Jesus (σινδών) further extends the interpretation; it is a death pall. At the tomb, the young man is clothed in a long robe (στολή). This garb is seen as a baptismal dress, thereby making the young man represent a catechumen who has been baptized into Jesus' death.[18] The fact that the Pauline writings provide similar baptismal imagery sustains the interpretation.

In Paul, we read such descriptions as the baptized as having "clothed" themselves "with Christ" (Gal 3:27), being "buried with [Christ] in baptism" to be raised with him "through faith in the power of God" (Col 2:12), throwing off "the works of darkness" and putting on "the armor of light" (Rom 13:11–14), and even putting away "the old self" of a "former way of life" (Eph 4:22–24). Although it is difficult if not impossible to prove that these passages are describing the earliest practices associated with the baptismal rite, they do reflect the double image of a believer discarding an old way of living in favor of a new.[19] In so doing, then, they support the understanding of baptism in the Markan passages in 10:46–52; 14:51–52; and 16:5.

The young man in the tomb instructs the women to tell Peter that the now-resurrected Jesus goes before them to Galilee, where they will be able to see him.

---

16. Lathrop, *Ground*, 10–11. See also Gordon Lathrop, *Holy People: A Liturgical Ecclesiology* (Minneapolis: Fortress, 1999), 176.

17. Lathrop, *Ground*, 10–11.

18. Ibid., 11.

19. See Giacomo Perego, *La nudità necessaria* (Milan: Edizioni San Paolo, 2000), 236–69, who develops the baptismal theme between 14:51–52 and 16:5 but does not connect it with Bartimaeus in 10:46–52.

The instruction to go to Galilee gives a theological meaning to these two geopolitical settings. Galilee represents the place of proclamation and manifestation, as we see in the first section of Jesus' ministry, and Jerusalem stands as the place of opposition and death. The women, however, remain for the time, at least, in Jerusalem, and there is nothing in the text to tell us that they follow any part of these instructions. Trembling, and in amazement, they flee. Their fear leaves them speechless, and Mark's Gospel abruptly ends here.

The Markan resurrection account reflects ambiguity over the emotional response of the women. Are they nearly paralyzed from fear, or are they held spellbound by awe? An investigation into three terms in the original Markan ending (16:1–8) helps to answer the question: τρόμος, ἔκστασις, and φοβέομαι. In the Markan Gospel, these three words occur together in the same verse only at 16:8. Previous to the resurrection account, the three terms, ἔκστασις, τρέμω, and φοβέομαι, appear in the two intercalated stories of Jairus's Daughter and the Woman with a Hemorrhage (5:21–43). The latter two terms are found as participles in Mark 5:33 and refer to the hemorrhaging woman, while ἔκστασις is paired with its cognate verb ἐξίστημι and describes the reaction of the household at the raising of Jairus's daughter in 5:42. In both cases, these three terms have only positive connotations; for the hemorrhaging woman and for Jairus's family, salvation has come to them through the ministry of Jesus. In neither instance do any of the persons involved flee the scene in fear and terror. This vocabulary and its use in the resurrection scene necessitate greater investigation.

The word pair φόβος and τρόμος appear elsewhere in the NT at 2 Cor 7.15, Eph 6:5; and Phil 2:12, where they instruct the reader on the proper way to approach Christ, and that stance is humility. Here, too, there is nothing to suggest abject fright. Both the Markan and Pauline uses of these terms arise specifically in the Wisdom tradition, but even the Pentateuch provides a support for their positive interpretation with its regular refrain of "fear of the Lord."[20] Furthermore, Leviticus and Deuteronomy utilize φόβος/φοβέομαι to express "revere" and "reverence" toward the Lord or his sanctuary.[21] For the Wisdom tradition and even for part of the prophetic tradition, however, "fear of the Lord" is a foundational component, and these two genres form the matrix for interpreting Mark's use of φοβέομαι.[22]

---

20. Or "fear of God." See in the LXX: Exod 14:31; Lev 19:14, 32; 25:17, 36, 43; Deut 4:10; 6:2, 13, 24; 8:6; 10:12, 20; 13:5; 14:23; 17:19; 31:12–13.

21. See in the LXX: Lev 19:3, 30; 26:2; Deut 28:58.

22. Or "fear of God." See in the LXX: Ps [110] 111:10; Prov 1:7; 9:10; 15:33; Sir 1:14, 16, 20, 27; 19:20; 21:11; Mic 6:9.

## Wisdom Tradition

In the Wisdom tradition, nearly all the examples of the phrase "fear of the Lord" employ the verb φοβέομαι or its cognates (in LXX).[23] In these instances, the concept "fear of the Lord" is not one of terror, confusion, or chaos. Rather, it signifies awe, wonder, and humility. Mark relies on this tradition for the interpretation of φόβος/φοβέομαι at the resurrection and at various points in the Gospel narrative.[24]

When Jesus walks on water (6:45–52), two verbs are used to describe the disciples' reaction. As Jesus first identifies himself, the disciples are terrified (φοβέομαι) (6:50). The disciples are amazed (ἐξίστημι), however, once Jesus is sitting in the boat (6:51). The fear and awe expressed by these two verbs are two complementary emotions. After Jesus steps from the water and into the bark, the fear that the disciples feel diminishes as the threat of the unknown turns to greater understanding of the benevolent force Jesus represents. In the next verse and with the verb πωρόω, however, Mark writes that the disciples hearts are hardened. A further complication is that this condition is somehow related to their lack of understanding over the feeding of the five thousand (6:34–44).

To "harden the heart" is a common phrase throughout the OT to portray opposition to the Lord, and in the LXX it is expressed by σκληρός/σκληρύνω.[25] Most of these occurrences fall in Exodus and describe Pharaoh's arrogance toward the Lord. The verb σκληρύνω and its cognate noun certainly mean "to harden," but it also has the connotation of "harsh" or "rough."

The Markan pericope ends with a perfect passive participle, ἀλλ᾿ ἦν αὐτῶν ἡ καρδία πεπωρωμένη. Furthermore, the verb πωρόω means "to harden" without any of the negative connotations signified by σκληρόω. Finally, the sequence in Mark is erratic. The disciples are afraid (6:50a), Jesus calms them (6:50b), and they are left completely astounded (6:51). After this resolution the reader then receives the information that the disciples had not understood the feeding of the five thousand; rather, their hearts were hardened (6:52). Two questions arise: Why were their hearts hardened at the miracle of the feeding? And why does Mark tell the reader this detail after the miracle of Jesus' walking on the water, especially after Jesus quells their fears to the point that they are absolutely astonished?

---

23. There are nearly 94 occurrences of εὐσέβεια and 14 of θεοσέβια/θεοσέβεια and their respective cognates throughout the LXX but without the genitive phrase "of the Lord." In these cases as well the general meaning of each is "piety," or "devotion."

24. See Marie Noonan Sabin, *Reopening the Word: Reading Mark as Theology in the Context of Early Judaism* (New York: Oxford University Press, 2002).

25. Exod 4:21; 7:3, 22; 8:15; 9:12, 35; 10:1, 20, 27; 11:10; 14:4, 8, 17; 2 Chr 36:13; 1 Esd 1:[46] 48; Ps [94] 95:8; Prov 28:14; Sir 3:26–27; Bar 2:30.

Many of the OT passages portraying the hardening of hearts are in the divine passive. This point is particularly true in Exodus, where the intention is to show that the Lord God and not Pharaoh is in control of the situation. Although there may be examples from the OT of the people hardening their own hearts,[26] Mark prefers to rely on the tradition of the divine passive and thus expresses the disciples' comportment in passive voice. The reason for such a choice in 6:52 is to offer a reason for the disciples' absolute astonishment in 6:51. In other words, the disciples are completely confused by everything they have seen and experienced even up to and including the feeding of the five thousand. When they see Jesus walk on the water and get into the boat, after first calming them with the words "Take courage, it is I, do not be afraid" (6:50), they begin to realize that he is no ordinary man; hence comes their astonishment.

Of all four Gospels, Mark goes to the greatest lengths in portraying the disciples as obtuse and dense when it comes to recognizing Jesus as the Messiah and Son of God, and we must be careful not to think that the moment of recognition at the walking on water constitutes a turning point in the disciples' reception of Jesus, for in Mark's narrative sequence there will be more examples of the disciples' lack of understanding. Indeed, after the second miraculous feeding, they still remain hard-hearted (8:17) and their understanding is called into question (8:21). Rather, in this fluctuation between faith and doubt, astonishment and impenetrability, we see the evangelist rendering an account of how Jesus' followers respond to his ministry. They and others to whom Jesus ministers have moments of recognition followed by moments of puzzlement.

Up to this point we have seen the Wisdom tradition's "fear of the Lord" in the reaction of the hemorrhaging woman and Jairus's household (5:21–43). At the walking on the water (6:45–52) this sense of awe inherent in the "fear of the Lord" comes over the disciples despite their being impervious to it in the feeding of the five thousand (6:34–44).

## *Fear and Awe*

At the calming of the storm (4:35–41), the disciples in the boat are awestruck at Jesus' miracle; ἐφοβήθησαν φόβον literally means "They feared a great fear" (4:41), or "They were deeply amazed and filled with awe." The disciples' awe in 4:41 is juxtaposed to their being absolutely terrified (δειλός) in 4:40. Although described after Jesus calms the wind and the waves, the context maintains that this terror is their reaction to a fierce storm, which causes water to pour in over the sides of the boat and sends them to call Jesus (4:38). While the storm is

---

26. Exod 9:35; 2 Chr 36:13; 1 Esd 1:[46] 48; Ps [94] 95:8.

raging, they are petrified with fear; after Jesus commands the elements to silence, they are exceedingly amazed, as their concluding question to each other confirms. Mark, then, distinguishes between the uncontrollable terror of δειλός in 4:40, and the awesome fear, which is the "fear of the Lord," in 4:41.

At the transfiguration, Mark again intensifies the grammatical construction by adding the prefix ἐκ to the adjective φόβος to describe the amazement the disciples feel at the sight of Moses, Elijah, with Jesus (9:6). The text states that Peter, James, and John are so terrified that they do not know what to say. Consequently, Peter's offer to construct three tents appears as the sputtering of a dumbfounded person struggling for words. They are simply awestruck. By contrast, in the conclusion to the healing of the Gerasene demoniac (5:15), Mark describes those who newly arrive as being terrified (φοβέομαι). Are they fearful of the demoniac, despite his having been healed, or are they fearful of the stranger from the other side of the lake who has just manifested this great power? The fact that the people beg Jesus to leave the territory suggests that they are as afraid of him as they had been of the demoniac. There is no mention of the disciples or their reaction to the event. Mark is comparing the disciples with the pagans in pagan territory. Despite Mark's proclivity toward showing the disciples in a negative light, there is not a single instance where any of them ask Jesus to depart.[27] Mark may portray them as lacking all understanding and sensitivity with regard to Jesus' ministry, and Jesus is always ready with a rebuke when they do, but the fact remains that they continue to follow him up until his arrest (14:50).

In ascending to Jerusalem, Mark uses φοβέομαι, but it is qualified by θαμβέομαι, "be amazed" or "shocked" (10:32). The writer is expressing two somewhat related but not synonymous terms to indicate that this band of disciples is both awe-filled and amazed over the fact that Jesus is displaying such determination to get to Jerusalem that he actually forges ahead without them. There has been a development that has led to this situation. In the second passion prediction (9:31–32), the disciples show their typical lack of understanding. Unlike the first passion prediction (8:31–33), where Peter contends with Jesus and suffers a harsh rebuke because of it, when Jesus repeats that he will be handed over, killed, and then rise, the disciples are afraid (φοβέομαι) to question him and remain silent, even though they do not understand the prediction (9:32). Immediately before Jesus makes his third passion prediction, it appears that the disciples, or at least some of them, fully understand the consequences, which explains both their amazement at his intrepidness and their own fear of what lies before them. After Jesus speaks of his passion, they once again remain silent.

---

27. But see Luke 5:8.

In the three remaining instances of φοβέομαι in Mark, the verb can only mean "to be afraid of, fearful." In Mark 11:18, 32; and 12:12, the chief priests, scribes, and then elders are afraid of Jesus as well as the crowds. There is nothing in these passages to suggest that these officials have any respect or awe toward either Jesus or the people.

When Mark uses φοβέομαι to describe the disciples, he implies a sense of awe, amazement, and humility; it signifies "fear of the Lord," which is so prevalent in the Wisdom tradition. The one possible exception to this conclusion is the employment of φοβέομαι at the second passion prediction (9:32). With the verb φοβέομαι at the resurrection, therefore, Mary Magdalene, Mary the mother James, and Salome are standing at the tomb in shock, awe, and reverence. Indeed, when they first enter the tomb and see the youth, they are "utterly amazed" (ἐκθαμβέομαι, 16:5) even as he tells them not to be (16:6). In the last verse of the original ending of Mark, the three terms τρόμος, ἔκστασις, and φοβέομαι all resurface and appear together for the first time since the 5:21–43 passage. We can conclude that the emotional state of the three women at the tomb is one of amazement, awe, and "fear of the Lord." It is certainly not intimidation or terror.[28]

## Interpretation of Mark's Resurrection Account

The remaining difficulty with this scene centers on the verb φεύγω. Not only does Mark say that the women leave the tomb, but the text also adds, as a way to intensify the situation, that they "flee" from it. The verb φεύγω appears five times in the Markan Gospel (5:14; 13:14; 14:50, 52; 16:8). With the exception of the resurrection narrative in 16:8, none of these verses show a predicate describing the emotional state of the subjects, although everything in the context points to them being frightened for their lives.[29] In Mark 16:8, however, this situation is not the case. They are not like the scared swineherds in Mark 5:14, fetching kith and kin to beg Jesus to leave the area. They are not fleeing "to the mountains" as Mark 13:14 warns. They are not like the terrified disciples or naked young man speeding away, fortified with the adrenalin of self-preservation. In fact, τρόμος and ἔκστασις are two modifiers describing the scene at Mark 16:8.

An important detail is that the women flee from the "tomb." Although Jesus is the first one laid in the kokim-style tomb, the whole area was a complex of tombs,

---

28. But see Paul Danove, "The Characterization and Narrative Function of the Women at the Tomb (Mark 15,40–41.47; 16,1–8)," *Bib* 77, no. 3 (1996): 374–97.

29. In Mark 5:14, the swineherds flee to the town and report the events. Since the people then come out and beg Jesus to leave their district (5:17), they are worried about their own lives and livelihoods.

some of which were newly hewn. The women were at the abode of cadavers, the dead. It is likely that Mark wants to underline this point. In the dispute with the Sadducees (12:18–27), Jesus makes a strong point that God "is not God of the dead but of the living" (12:27). The women go to the tomb to anoint a dead body, yet they encounter a lively youth dressed in white, sitting near where the corpse ought to be. Mark is proclaiming that death is dead, so there is no need to waste time in tombs. Indeed, if other Gospel narratives are in any way indicative of early Christian belief, the Lukan resurrection account, posing the very question, shows two men inside the tomb asking the women, "Why do you seek the living one among the dead?" (Luke 24:5).

Mary Magdalene, Mary the mother of James, and Salome are so overawed that they are speechless, despite the charge to tell the disciples and Peter what they have seen and heard. Drawing on the Markan portrayal of Jesus' renown during his earthly ministry, despite his constant command to silence in the face of his expelling demons and healing, it is probable that Mark does not intend the reader to conclude that the three women remain silent indefinitely. What Mark wants to present through the experience of Mary Magdalene, the other Mary, and Salome is the fear of *mysterium tremendum et fascinans* before the living God.

The women disciples, unlike their male counterparts, had the ability to observe every detail of Jesus' death and burial without raising the authorities' suspicion. For all their efforts, however, they appear to many as being no more successful than the men in understanding Jesus' message. Maybe a better interpretation is that the women understood the whole Jesus event, the kerygma, all too well, hence their nearly catatonic amazement in 16:8. They see that Jesus' passion, death, and resurrection have remade creation.

The young man at the tomb, representing the glory that all disciples have a share in, tells the women to go to Galilee, for there they will see Jesus, just as Jesus himself had told them (16:7). In Mark, Galilee is where Jesus commenced his whole earthly mission. Thus we see a cyclical aspect to Mark's Gospel. Why does Jesus go to Galilee, however? Why must the disciples go there? Will he be any different now than when he first began?

When Jesus himself instructs the disciples that he will go before them to Galilee, it is within the context of the passion narrative, specifically his fore-telling Peter's denial (14:27–31). The return to Galilee completes a circle, but it is a circle that has been broken by the resurrection of the "Son of Man." In nearly every case where Jesus speaks about himself as the "Son of Man," there is always some reference to his passion or resurrection.[30] In the apocalyptic discourse and

---

30. The only exceptions are Mark 2:10, 28.

then at the trial, Jesus stresses the triumphant character of the Son of Man, who will be "coming in the clouds with great power and glory" (13:26; 14:62).

By completing the circle in going to Galilee, therefore, Jesus completes the redemption of the world. The disciples, who followed him in Galilee and to Jerusalem, now follow him into glory back to Galilee. Jesus will never again be debased, and Mark tells us that the disciples who follow him to the cross will not be either. For this reason, the women at the tomb are awestruck.

This story would sound remarkable to the first-century Christians and those whom they were trying to evangelize. For Jewish Christians, there would be the benefit of drawing upon a whole tradition that shows God working in human history. The universalist dimensions of Judaism, as represented by readings such as Isa 60:1–3, would give a particularly helpful background for interpreting the kerygma.

Mark's Gospel, with its special attention to the tearing of the heavens at the baptism and the rending of the temple veil at Jesus' death, would lend itself to viewing the cosmic character of Christ's redemption. Such a cosmic understanding is evident in the Pauline writings. The question now is whether Gentile Christians would have had a comparable or even an overextending concept of a cosmic divinity allying itself to human beings. This study suggests that it did, and Paul is responsible for importing it into the Christian community at Rome.

# Chapter 9

# Conclusion

## Summary

The tearing open of the heavens at the baptism (1:10) symbolizes God breaking through to creation. Jesus' scream from the cross is creation's reply, and the rending of the temple veil shows the effect of that cry (15:34, 38). The transfiguration manifests to the disciples what the Father states to Jesus at the baptism. This rending of the heavens resonates with both Jewish and Gentile concepts and understanding of the created world.

In Mark, Jesus' death on the cross is the culmination of the battle with Satan. Jesus the Son of God also represents creation. Because he becomes a victim of sin and death and recognizes the despair such sin brings, he rescues creation from death. The splayed temple curtain represents God's redemptive action brought about by Jesus' subjection to the darkness of sin. In Mark's Gospel, God is not found in the temple but at the cross; that is where the disciple will find him.

The three women to whom the youth at the tomb announces Jesus' resurrection remain silent from awe rather than from fear or lack of faith. The instruction to meet the resurrected Jesus in Galilee completes a circle of life, death, and return to life, thereby giving the resurrection a cosmic character strongly reminiscent of Paul's writings.

If the disciple sees God at the cross, that cross leads to the resurrection. The cross is a prominent feature in the Gospel of Mark. To become a disciple is to walk the same path that Jesus trod. This whole process is signaled by the baptism, with its divine communication and actions of descent and ascent, a strong Pauline concept.

The Bartimaeus pericope focuses on "blindness," "Son of David," "see again," and "follow." The name "Bartimaeus" serves to challenge the whole worldview set out in Plato's *Timaeus*: by his free act of discipleship, Bartimaeus connects the Son of David to the Son of God.

The Markan presentation of Jesus' death, the climax of the narrative, brings the act of divine communication full circle. At the baptism, God communicates to creation, and with Jesus' cry from the cross, creation replies. The rending of the temple curtain signals the communication in symbols recognizable to both Jew and Gentile. The women at the tomb are so awestruck that they do not tell anyone what they have witnessed. The notice to meet Jesus in Galilee is an affirmation of the resurrection by moving from the place of the dead (the tomb) to the land of the living (Galilee), thus rejoining Paul's cosmic theology, which moves from life to death, and back to eternal life.

We have seen how the Hellenistic cosmology is evident in several key Markan passages. Consequently, with such an understanding so important for the evangelist, this theme is present in other parts of the Gospel as well.

## Conclusion

Although Mithraism and Christianity grew in the same Hellenistic soil, the important point is that Christianity differs from Mithraism in its soteriology. Unlike Mithraism and indeed unlike all mystery cults, Christianity's followers participate in the life of their God; they are not mere observers imitating their deity and depending on that god's capricious beneficence for salvation.

In the Greco-Roman world during the intertestamental period, Plato's *Timaeus* was the currency of the religious, scientific, and philosophical realm. Its astronomical calculation that the whole cosmos was a living entity forming a cross at the intersection of two ecliptics combined with Posidonius of Tarsus' teaching on astral immortality. The cult of Mithras, at this stage in its development in Tarsus of Cilicia, molded with the vision of the universe outlined in Plato's *Timaeus*. Together, these two systems provided for Paul a worthy vehicle to become the apostle to the Gentiles. Not only was he able to speak to the world on its own terms, but he was also able to engage the participation in the life of a god that Mithraism proclaimed. He was also able to offer something better in Christ.

In Mark's Gospel, the portrayal of Christ's struggle against Satan is given a cosmological thrust. Through his death and resurrection, Jesus is victorious over the diabolical foe. We have discussed how a disciple participates in Christ's victory through baptism. What we are asserting here is that Mark's cosmology employs the same understanding, thought, and construction as the Mithraic belief system does. Was it Paul's influence on the church at Rome which made it so?

Even though Mithraism did not flourish in the city of Rome until after Mark's Gospel was written, it was introduced into the empire through its eastern doors; that circumstance put it into direct contact with Paul. Paul uses Mithraic cosmological concepts to explain Christ's role in the cosmos. Markan theology also has an overarching worldview with strong Mithraic echoes and currents. At this point, it is impossible to ascertain how, when, and where Paul influenced the Markan *text*, if at all. The most we can say is that Paul's writings and Mark's

Gospel share the same worldview, and consequently we can understand how the earliest converts heard the Christian message. With certainty, we can also say that there are no contradictions in how the apostle and the evangelist each viewed Christ's redemptive act. We can also speculate with some surety that between the Pauline and Markan writings, the proclamation of the Gospel was equipped to adopt and adapt a major scientific, religious, and philosophical system and use it for the evangelization of the Roman world.

For this reason, Mark's Gospel rings with a strong Pauline cord. Its emphasis on a discipleship that demands descent with Christ in baptism to rise with him at the resurrection reflects the Mithraic pattern of humiliation and exaltation. By naming the blind man at Jericho "Bartimaeus," Mark takes the whole Hellenistic universe and turns it upside down. Mark is saying that Timaeus is blind until he sees Christ. Yes, the universe is held together by a cross, but it is the cross of Christ. Yes, there is immortality, but something greater than immortality: eternal life.

With such a vision and promise, disciples can only stand speechless and trembling in awe, as the women do in the garden of the resurrection. Christ's disciples also inherit this eternal life in which they will dwell with the Lord of the cosmos infused with the divine love and unbounded by time, space, suffering, and death.

# Bibliography

Andersen, F. I., trans. *2 (Slavonic Apocalypse of) Enoch.* In *OTP* 1:91–221.

Andreussi, M. "Mitra (S. Prisca; Reg. XIII)." *LTUR* 3:268–69.

Ascough, Richard S. *What Are They Saying about the Formation of Pauline Churches?* New York: Paulist Press, 1998.

Bausani, Alessandro. "Note sulla preistoria astronomica del mito di Mithra." Pages 503–15 in *Mysteria Mithrae.* Edited by Ugo Bianchi. Leiden: Brill, 1980.

Beck, Roger L. "Cautes and Cautopates: Some Astronomical Considerations." *JMS* 1, no. 2 (1976): 10.

———. Lecture: "Exaltation/Humiliation: Coding in Word and Image in Mithraism, Ancient Astrology, and Early Christianity." Toronto, ON: SBL Annual Meeting, Nov. 24, 2002.

———. "A Note on the Scorpion in the Tauroctony." *JMS* 1, no. 2 (1976): 209.

Betz, Hans Dieter. "The Mithras Inscriptions of Santa Prisca and the New Testament." *NovT* 10, no. 1 (January 1968): 62–80.

Blackburn, Barry. "Theios anēr and the Markan Miracle Traditions." WUNT 40. Tübingen: Mohr (Siebeck), 1991.

Boismard, M.-É. *L'Évangile de Marc: Sa préhistoire.* ÉBib 26. Paris: J. Gabalda, 1994.

Boman, Thorleif. "Das letzte Wort Jesu." *ST* 17 (1963): 103–19.

Bousset, Wilhelm. *Kyrios Christos.* Nashville: Abingdon, 1970.

Brown, Raymond. *The Death of the Messiah.* Vol. 2. New York: Doubleday, 1994.

Bultmann, Rudolf. *Die Geschicte der synoptischen Tradition.* Göttingen: Vandenhoeck & Ruprecht, 1957.

———. *Primitive Christianity in Its Contemporary Setting.* London: Thames & Hudson, 1956.

Bury, R. G., trans. *Plato,* vol. 9, *Timaeus, Critias, Cleitophon, Menexenus, Epistles.* LCL. Cambridge, MA: Harvard University Press, 1989.

Caronna, E. Lissi. "Castra Peregrina." *LTUR* 1:249–50.

———. "Castra Peregrina: Mithraeum." *LTUR* 1:251.

Charlesworth, J. H., trans. *Treatise of Shem.* In *OTP* 1:473–86.

Clauss, Manfred. *The Roman Cult of Mithras: The God and His Mysteries.* Translated by Richard Gordon. New York: Routledge, 2000.

Culpepper, R. Alan. "Why Mention the Garment?" *JBL* 101, no. 1 (March 1982): 131–32.

Cumont, Franz. *The Mysteries of Mithra.* New York: Dover, 1956.

Danove, Paul. "The Characterization and Narrative Function of the Women at the Tomb (Mark 15,40–41.47; 16,1–8)." *Bib* 77, no. 3 (1996): 374–97.

della Giovampaola, I. "Mitra (S. Clemens; Reg. II)." *LTUR* 3:257–59.

Dibelius, Martin. *From Tradition to Gospel.* London: Nicholson and Watson, 1934.

Donahue, John R. *Are You the Christ? The Trial Narrative in the Gospel of Mark.* SBLDS 10. Missoula, MT: Society of Biblical Literature, 1973.

Donahue, John R., and Daniel J. Harrington. *The Gospel of Mark.* SP 2. Collegeville, MN: Liturgical Press, 2002.

Douglas, Mary. *Purity and Danger: An Analysis of the Concepts of Pollution and Taboos.* London: Routledge & Kegan Paul, 1966.

Dunn, James D. G. *Christology in the Making.* Grand Rapids: Eerdmans, 1989.

1 *Enoch.* See Isaac, E.

2 *Enoch.* See Andersen, F. I.

Falls, Thomas B., trans. *Dialogue with Trypho.* Selections from Fathers of the Church 3. Washington: Catholic University Press, 2003.

———, trans. *Saint Justin Martyr.* New York: Christian Heritage, 1965.

Feldman, Louis H., trans. *Josephus,* vol. 10, *Jewish Antiquities: Book 20; Index.* LCL. Cambridge, MA: Harvard University Press, 1965.

Gressmann, Hugo. *Die orientalischen Religionen im hellenistisch-römischen Zeitalter.* Berlin: de Gruyter, 1930.

*Guida d'Italia del Touring Club Italiano.* Milan: Artistico-Letteraria del T.C.I., 1979.

Gysens, J. Calzini. "Aedes Herculis et Dionysii." *LTUR* 3:262.

———. "Arx." *LTUR* 3:265–66.

———. "Domus Augustana." *LTUR* 3:266.

———. "Domus: Nummi." *LTUR* 3:262.

———. "Emporium." *LTUR* 3:270.

———. "Facoltà di Ingegneria." *LTUR* 3:260.

———. "Horti Lamiani." *LTUR* 3:261.

———. "Horti Sallustiani." *LTUR* 3:264.

———. "M. degli Olympii, S. Silvestro in Capite." *LTUR* 3:264–65.

———. "Mithra." *LTUR* 3:257.

———. "Ospedale di San Giovanni sul Celio." *LTUR* 3:261–62.

———. "Palazzo Barberini." *LTUR* 3:263–64.

———. "Palazzo della Cancelleria Apostolica." *LTUR* 3:266.

———. "S. Saba." *LTUR* 3:269.

———. "Spelaeum in Via G. Lanza." *LTUR* 3:260–61.

———. "Spelaeum nel Foro di Nerva." *LTUR* 3:265.

———. "Thermae Titi." *LTUR* 3:260.

———. "Via Mazzarino." *LTUR* 3:263.

———. "Via Passalacqua." *LTUR* 3:259–60.

———. "Vigna Muti." *LTUR* 3:262–63.

———. "Vigne e Magarozzi." *LTUR* 3:259.

———. "Villa Giustiniani-Massimo." *LTUR* 3:261.

Haufe, Günther. "Die Mysterien." In *Umwelt des Urchristentums,* vol. 1. *Darstellung des neutestamentlichen Zeitalters.* Edited by J. Leipoldt and W. Grundmann. Berlin: Evangelische Verlagsanstalt, 1975.

Hilgert, Earle. "The Son of Timaeus: Blindness, Sight, Ascent, Vision in Mark." In *Reimagining Christian Origins.* Edited by Elizabeth Castelli and Hal Taussig. Valley Forge, PA: Trinity Press International, 1996.

Holmes, Michael W., ed. *The Apostolic Fathers: Greek Texts and English Translations.* Grand Rapids: Baker Books, 1999.

Humphrey, Hugh M. *He Is Risen! A New Reading of Mark's Gospel.* New York: Paulist Press, 1992.

Insler, Stanley. "A New Interpretation of the Bull-Slaying Motif." Pages 519–38 in *Hommages à Maarten J. Vermaseren.* Edited by M. B. de Boer and T. A. Edridge. Leiden: Brill, 1978.

Isaac, E., trans. *1 Enoch.* In *OTP* 1:13–89.

Jeremias, Joachim. "Μωυσῆς." *TDNT* 4 (1967): 848–73.

Johnson, Earl S., Jr. "Mark 10:46–52: Blind Bartimaeus." *CBQ* 40 (1978): 191–204.

Josephus. *A.J.:* Books 5–14. See Marcus, Ralph.

———. *A.J.:* Books 18–20. See Feldman, Louis H.

———. *B.J.:* Books 1–7. See Thackeray, H. St. J.

Justin Martyr. See Falls, Thomas B.

Kertelge, Kurt. *Die Wunder Jesu im Markusevangelium: Eine redaktionsgeschichte Untersuchung.* Munich: Kösel, 1970.

Knibb, M. A., trans. *Martyrdom and Ascension of Isaiah.* In *OTP* 2:143–76.

Lathrop, Gordon. "Biblical and Liturgical Reorientation in the World." *Worship* 77, no. 1 (January 2003): 2–22.

———. *Holy Ground: A Liturgical Cosmology.* Minneapolis: Fortress, 2003.

———. *Holy People: A Liturgical Ecclesiology.* Minneapolis: Fortress, 1999.

Lease, Gary. "Mithraism and Christianity: Borrowings and Transformations." *ANRW,* Part 2, *Principat,* 23.2 (1980): 1306–32.

Lega, C. "S. Sabina." *LTUR* 3:269–70.

Loisy, Alfred. *Les mystère païens et le mystère chrétien.* Paris: Emile Nourry, 1914.

Malina, Bruce J. *The New Testament World: Insights from Cultural Anthropology.* Atlanta: John Knox, 1981.

Marcus, Ralph, trans. Josephus, vols. 5–7. Jewish Antiquities, Books 5–14; LCL. Cambridge, MA: Harvard University Press, 1935–1943.

Martin, Ralph P. *A Hymn of Christ: Philippians 2:5–11 in Recent Interpretation and in the Setting of Early Christian Worship.* Downers Grove, IL: InterVarsity, 1997.

Metzger, Bruce M. "Methodology in the Study of the Mystery Religions and Early Christianity." Pages 1–24 in *Historical and Literary Studies: Pagan, Jewish, and Christian.* NTTS 8. Grand Rapids: Eerdmans, 1968.

Murphy-O'Connor, Jerome. "Crucifixion in the Pauline Letters." In *The Cross in the Christian Tradition.* Edited by Elizabeth Dreyer. New York: Paulist Press, 2000.

Nelis, Jan. "God and Heaven in the Old Testament." Pages 22–33 in *Heaven.* Edited by Bas van Iersel and Edward Schillebeeckx. Concilium: Religion in the Seventies. New York: Seabury, 1979.

Nineham, Dennis, E. *Saint Mark.* Philadelphia, PA: Westminster Press, 1978.

Nock, A. D. "Early Gentile Christianity and Its Hellenistic Background." Pages 49–133 in *Essays on Religion and the Ancient World.* Edited by Zeph Stewart. Cambridge, MA: Harvard University Press, 1972.

———. "Hellenistic Mysteries and Christian Sacraments." Pages 791–820 in *Essays on Religion and the Ancient World.* Edited by Zeph Stewart. Cambridge, MA: Harvard University Press, 1972.

———. "The Vocabulary of the New Testament." Pages 341–47 in *Essays on Religion and the Ancient World.* Edited by Zeph Stewart. Cambridge, MA: Harvard University Press, 1972.

Nodet, Etienne, and Justin Taylor. *The Origins of Christianity: An Exploration.* Collegeville, MN: Liturgical Press, 1998.

Origen. *Contra Celsum.* Translated by Henry Chadwick. New York: Cambridge University Press, 1980.

Patella, Michael, *The Death of Jesus*. CahRB 43. Paris: J. Gabalda, 1999.

Perego, Giacomo. *La nudità necessaria*. Milan: Edizioni San Paolo, 2000.

Piranomante, M. "Spelunga." *LTUR* 3:267–68.

Plato. See Bury, R. B.

Ramieri, A. M. "Antrum." *LTUR* 3:266–67.

Reitzenstein, Richard. *Hellenistic Mystery-Religions: Their Basic Ideas and Significance.* Translated by John E. Steely. Pittsburgh: Pickwick, 1978.

Robbins, Vernon K. "The Healing of Blind Bartimaeus (10:46–52) in the Marcan Theology." *JBL* 92 (1973): 224–83.

Sabin, Marie Noonan. *Reopening the Word: Reading Mark as Theology in the Context of Early Judaism.* New York: Oxford University Press, 2002.

Såhlin, Harald. "Mk 15,34." *Bib* 33 (1952): 62–66.

Schmid, Josef. *The Gospel according to Mark.* Staten Island, NY: Alba, 1968.

Soler, Jean. "Semiotique de la nourriture dans la Bible." *Annales Économies, sociétés, civilizations* 28, no. 4 (1973): 943–55.

Speidel, Michael. *Mithras-Orion.* Leiden: Brill, 1980.

Stark, Karl B. *Zwei Mithräen der grossherzoglichen Alterthümersammlung in Karlsruhe.* Heidelberg, 1865.

Suetonius. *The Twelve Caesars.* Translated by Robert Graves. New York: Penguin, 1979.

Taylor, Justin. "The Coming of Elijah, Mt 17:10–13 and Mk 9:11–13: The Development of the Texts." *RB* 98 (1991): 107–19.

Taylor, Vincent. *The Gospel according to St. Mark.* 2nd ed. London: Macmillan, 1966.

Tertullian. *De baptismo.* Translated by Ernest Evans. London: SPCK, 1964.

———. *De corona.* Edited by Jacques Fontaine. Paris: Presses Universitaires de France, 1966.

———. *Praescriptione haereticoram.* Edited by Erwin Preuschen. Frankfurt: Minerva, 1968.

Thackeray, H. St. J., trans. Josephus, vol. 2. *Jewish War*, Books 1–3; LCL. New York: G. P. Putnam's Sons, 1927.

———, trans. Josephus, vol. 3. *Jewish War*, Books 4–7; LCL. New York: G.@P. Putnam's Sons, 1928.

Ulansey, David. *The Origins of the Mithraic Mysteries.* New York: Oxford University Press, 1989.

Vermaseren, Maarten J. *Mithras, Geschichte eines Kultes.* Stuttgart: W. Kohlhammer, 1965.

Wagner, Günther. *Pauline Baptism and the Pagan Mysteries: The Problem of the Pauline Doctrine of Baptism in Romans VI, 1–11, in the Light of Its Religio-Historical "Parallels."* Edinburgh: Oliver & Boyd, 1967.

Wedderburn, A. J. M. *Baptism and Resurrection: Studies in Pauline Theology against Its Graeco-Roman Background.* WUNT 44. Tübingen: Mohr (Siebeck), 1987.

———. "Hellenistic Christian Traditions in Romans 6?" *NTS* 29 (1983): 337–55.

———. "Paul and the Hellenistic Mystery-Cults: On Posing the Right Questions." Pages 817–33 in *La soteriologia dei culti orientali nell'Impero romano: Atti dei Colloquio internazionale su la soteriologia dei culti orientali nell'Impero romano, Roma 24–28 Settembre 1979.* Edited by Ugo Bianchi and Maarten J. Vermaseren. ÉPRO 92. Leiden: Brill, 1982.

———. "The Soteriology of the Mysteries and Pauline Baptismal Theology." *NovT* 29 (1987): 53–72.

Wright, J. Edward. *The Early History of Heaven.* New York: Oxford University Press, 2000.

# Index